The
TREASURE
PRINCIPLE

LifeChange Books

RANDY
ALCORN

Multnomah Books

The author wants to acknowledge his editor, James Lund:
Thanks, Jim, for your servant's heart and your
valued partnership on this project.

THE TREASURE PRINCIPLE
published by Multnomah Books

© 2001 by Eternal Perspective Ministries
International Standard Book Number: 978-1-59052-508-1

Cover design by Kirk DouPonce, DogEaredDesign.com
Cover image by Dog Eared Design, LLC

Scripture quotations are from:
The Holy Bible, New International Version © 1973, 1984 by International
Bible Society, used by permission of Zondervan Publishing House
New American Standard Bible (NASB) © 1960, 1977 by the Lockman Foundation
The Holy Bible, New King James Version (NKJV) © 1984 by Thomas Nelson, Inc.
The Holy Bible, English Standard Version (ESV)
© 2001 by Crossway Bibles, a division of Good News Publishers.
Used by permission. All rights reserved.

Published in the United States by WaterBrook Multnomah, an imprint of the Crown
Publishing Group, a division of Random House Inc., New York.

MULTNOMAH and its mountain colophon are registered trademarks of Random House Inc.

Printed in the United States of America

The song "Thank You" was copyrighted in 1988 by Gaither Music/ASCAP.
It was performed by Ray Boltz on the 2001 album titled *Moments for the Heart:
The Very Best of Ray Boltz Volume 1 & 2.*

For information:
MULTNOMAH BOOKS
12265 ORACLE BOULEVARD, SUITE 200 • COLORADO SPRINGS, CO 80921

Library of Congress Cataloging-in-Publication Data:
Alcorn, Randy C.
  The treasure principle: discovering the secret of joyful giving / by
Randy Alcorn.
    p. cm.
Includes bibliographical references.
ISBN 1-59052-508-6
    1-57673-780-2
1. Wealth—Religious aspects—Christianity. I. Title
BR115.W4 A44 2001
241'.68—dc21   2001004393

11 12 13—55

Table of Contents

INTRODUCTION

All your life, you've been on a treasure hunt. You've been searching for a perfect person and a perfect place. Jesus is that person; heaven is that place. So if you're a Christian, you've already met the person, and you're already headed to the place.

But there's a problem. You're not yet living with that person, and you're not yet living in that place!

You may attend church regularly, pray, and read the Bible. But life can still be drudgery, can't it? You dutifully put one foot in front of the other, plodding across the hot, barren ground, longing for a joy you cannot find, a treasure that eludes you.

Jesus told a story like that. It's about a hidden treasure that, once discovered, brings life-changing joy. But before we get started on our little journey, I want you to know something. Some books try to motivate giving out of guilt. This isn't one of them.

This book is about something else—the joy of giving. The Treasure Principle has long been buried. It's time to unearth it. It's a simple yet profound idea—with radical implications. Once you grasp it and put it into practice, nothing will ever look the same. And believe me, you won't want it to.

When you discover the secret joy of the Treasure Principle, I guarantee you'll never be content with less.

Chapter 1

BURIED TREASURE

*He is no fool who gives what he cannot keep
to gain what he cannot lose.*

JIM ELLIOT

A first-century Hebrew walks alone on a hot afternoon, staff in hand. His shoulders are stooped, sandals covered with dirt, tunic stained with sweat. But he doesn't stop to rest. He has pressing business in the city.

He veers off the road into a field, seeking a shortcut. The owner won't mind—travelers are permitted this courtesy. The field is uneven. To keep his balance he thrusts his staff into the dirt.

Thunk. The staff strikes something hard.

He stops, wipes his brow, and pokes again.

Thunk. Something's under there, and it's not a rock.

The weary traveler tells himself that he can't afford to

linger. But his curiosity won't let him go. He jabs at the ground. Something reflects a sliver of sunlight. He drops to his knees and starts digging.

Five minutes later, he's uncovered it—a case fringed in gold. By the looks of it, it's been there for decades. Heart racing, he pries off the rusty lock and opens the lid.

Gold coins! Jewelry! Precious stones of every color! A treasure more valuable than anything he's ever imagined.

Hands shaking, the traveler inspects the coins, issued in Rome over seventy years ago. Some wealthy man must have buried the case and died suddenly, the secret of the treasure's location dying with him. There is no homestead nearby. Surely the current landowner has no clue that the treasure's here. (By the way, parables have one central purpose. The point of this one is not to command taking advantage of a landowner's ignorance, but to respond joyfully at finding buried treasure.)

The traveler closes the lid, buries the chest, and marks the spot. He turns around, heading home—only now he's not plodding. He's skipping like a little boy, smiling broadly.

What a find! Unbelievable! I've got to have that treasure! But I can't just take it—that would be stealing. Whoever owns the field owns what's in it. But how can I afford to buy it? I'll sell my farm...and crops...all my tools...my prize oxen. Yes, if I sell everything, that should be enough!

From the moment of his discovery, the traveler's life changes. The treasure captures his imagination, becomes the stuff of his dreams. It's his reference point, his new center of gravity. The traveler takes every new step with this treasure in mind. He experiences a radical paradigm shift.

This story is captured by Jesus in a single verse: "The kingdom of heaven is like treasure hidden in a field. When a man found it, he hid it again, and then in his joy went and sold all he had and bought that field" (Matthew 13:44).

Some believe this passage speaks of people finding the treasure of Christ and His kingdom. Many believe it speaks of Jesus giving His life to obtain the treasure of the subjects and kingdom He rules. In either case, it certainly envisions the joy of finding great and eternal treasure that far surpasses the costs to obtain it.

As we will see, the biblical basis for the treasure principle is not this passage, but Matthew 6:19–21. Nevertheless, Matthew 13:44 serves as a vivid picture of the joy of surrendering lesser treasures to find greater ones.

God sees our faith and finances as inseparable.

THE MONEY CONNECTION

The parable of hidden treasure is one of many references and illustrations Jesus made using money and possessions. In fact, 15 percent of everything Christ said relates to this topic—more than His teachings on heaven and hell combined.

Why did Jesus put such an emphasis on money and possessions?

Because there's a fundamental connection between our spiritual lives and how we think about and handle money. We may try to divorce our faith and our finances, but God sees them as inseparable.

Years ago I came to this realization on an airplane while reading Luke 3. John the Baptist is preaching to crowds of people who've gathered to hear him and be baptized. Three different groups ask him what they should do to bear the fruit of repentance. John gives three answers:

1. Everyone should share clothes and food with the poor (v. 11).
2. Tax collectors shouldn't pocket extra money (v. 13).
3. Soldiers should be content with their wages and not extort money (v. 14).

Each answer relates to money and possessions. But no one asked John about that! They asked what they should do to demonstrate the fruit of spiritual transformation. So why didn't John talk about other things?

Sitting there on that airplane, I realized that our

approach to money and possessions isn't just important—it's central to our spiritual lives. It's of such high priority to God that John the Baptist couldn't talk about spirituality without talking about how to handle money and possessions.

The same thing began to jump out at me in other passages. Zacchaeus said to Jesus, "Look, Lord! Here and now I give half of my possessions to the poor, and if I have cheated anybody out of anything, I will pay back four times the amount" (Luke 19:8).

Jesus' response? "Today salvation has come to this house" (v. 9). Zacchaeus's radical new approach to money proved that his heart had been transformed.

Then there were the Jerusalem converts who eagerly sold their possessions to give to the needy (Acts 2:45; 4:32–35). And the Ephesian occultists, who proved their conversion was authentic when they burned their magic books, worth what today would be millions of dollars (Acts 19:19).

The poor widow steps off the pages of Scripture by giving two small coins. Jesus praised her: "She, out of her poverty, put in everything" (Mark 12:44).

In stark contrast, Jesus spoke of a rich man who spent all his wealth on himself. He planned to tear down his barns and build larger ones, storing up for himself so he could retire early and take life easy.

But God called the man a fool, saying, "This very night your life will be demanded from you. Then who will get what you have prepared for yourself?" (Luke 12:20).

The greatest indictment against him—and the proof of his spiritual condition—is that he was rich toward himself, but not rich toward God.

When a rich young man pressed Jesus about how to gain eternal life, Jesus told him, "Sell your possessions and give to the poor, and you will have treasure in heaven. Then come, follow me" (Matthew 19:21). The man was obsessed with earthly treasures. Jesus called him to something higher—heavenly treasures.

Jesus knew that money and possessions were the man's god. He realized that the man wouldn't serve God unless he dethroned his money idol. But the seeker considered the price too great. Sadly, he walked away from real treasures.

SMART OR STUPID?

This young man wasn't willing to give up everything for a greater treasure, but our traveler in the field was. Why? Because the traveler understood what it would gain him.

Do you feel sorry for the traveler? After all, his discovery cost him everything. But we aren't to pity this man;

we're to *envy* him! His sacrifice pales in comparison to his reward. Consider the costs-to-benefits ratio—the benefits far outweigh the costs.

The traveler made short-term sacrifices to obtain a long-term reward. "It cost him everything he owned," you might lament. Yes, *but it gained him everything that mattered.*

If we miss the phrase "in his joy," we miss everything. The man wasn't exchanging lesser treasures for greater treasures out of dutiful drudgery but out of joyful exhilaration. He would have been a fool not to do exactly what he did.

Christ's story about treasure in the field is an object lesson concerning heavenly treasure. Of course, no matter how great the value of that earthly fortune, it would be worthless in eternity. In fact, it's exactly this kind of treasure that people waste their lives pursuing. Jesus is appealing to what we *do* value—temporary, earthly treasure—in order to make an analogy about what we *should* value—eternal, heavenly treasure.

David spoke of such treasure: "I rejoice in your promise like one who finds great spoil" (Psalm 119:162). God's promises are eternal treasures, and discovering them brings great joy.

In Matthew 6, Jesus fully unveils the foundation of what I call the Treasure Principle. It's one of His most-neglected teachings:

"Do not store up for yourselves treasures on earth, where moth and rust destroy, and where thieves break in and steal. But store up for yourselves treasures in heaven, where moth and rust do not destroy, and where thieves do not break in and steal. For where your treasure is, there your heart will be also." (Matthew 6:19–21)

Consider what Jesus is saying: "Do not store up for yourselves treasures on earth." Why not? Because earthly treasures are bad? No. *Because they won't last.*

Scripture says, "Cast but a glance at riches, and they are gone, for they will surely sprout wings and fly off to the sky like an eagle" (Proverbs 23:5). What a picture. Next time you buy a prized possession, imagine it sprouting wings and flying off. Sooner or later it will disappear.

> *Storing up earthly treasures isn't simply wrong. It's just plain stupid.*

But when Jesus warns us not to store up treasures on earth, it's not just because wealth *might* be lost; it's because wealth will *always* be lost. Either it leaves us while we live, or we leave it when we die. No exceptions.

Imagine you're alive at the end of the Civil War. You're

living in the South, but you are a Northerner. You plan to move home as soon as the war is over. While in the South you've accumulated lots of Confederate currency. Now, suppose you know for a fact that the North is going to win the war and the end is imminent. *What will you do with your Confederate money?*

If you're smart, there's only one answer. You should immediately cash in your Confederate currency for U.S. currency—the only money that will have value once the war is over. Keep only enough Confederate currency to meet your short-term needs.

As a Christian, you have inside knowledge of an eventual worldwide upheaval caused by Christ's return. This is the ultimate insider trading tip: Earth's currency will become worthless when Christ returns—or when you die, whichever comes first. (And either event could happen at any time.)

Investment experts known as market timers read signs that the stock market is about to take a downward turn, then recommend switching funds immediately into more dependable vehicles such as money markets, treasury bills, or certificates of deposit.

Jesus functions here as the foremost market timer. He tells us to once and for all switch investment vehicles. He instructs us to transfer our funds from earth (which is volatile and ready to take a permanent dive) to heaven (which is totally dependable, insured by God Himself, and is coming soon to forever replace earth's economy). Christ's financial forecast for earth is bleak—but He's unreservedly bullish about investing in heaven, where every market indicator is eternally positive!

There's nothing wrong with Confederate money, as long as you understand its limits. Realizing its value is temporary should radically affect your investment strategy. To accumulate vast earthly treasures that you can't possibly hold on to for long is equivalent to stockpiling Confederate money even though you know it's about to become worthless.

God expects us to act out of enlightened self-interest.

According to Jesus, storing up earthly treasures isn't simply wrong. It's just plain stupid.

A TREASURE MENTALITY

Jesus doesn't just tell us where *not* to put our treasures. He also gives the best investment advice you'll ever hear: "Store up for yourselves treasures in heaven" (Matthew 6:20).

If you stopped reading too soon, you would have thought Christ was against our storing up treasures for ourselves. No. He's all for it! In fact, He *commands* it. Jesus has a treasure mentality. He *wants* us to store up treasures. He's just telling us to stop storing them in the wrong place and start storing them in the right place!

"Store up *for yourselves.*" Doesn't it seem strange that Jesus commands us to do what's in our own best interests? Wouldn't that be selfish? No. God expects and commands us to act out of enlightened self-interest. He wants us to live to His glory, but what is to His glory is always to our good. As John Piper puts it, "God is most glorified in us when we are most satisfied in Him."

Selfishness is when we pursue gain at the expense of others. But God doesn't have a limited number of treasures to distribute. When you store up treasures for yourself in heaven, it doesn't reduce the treasures available to others. In fact, it is by serving God and others that we store up heavenly treasures. Everyone gains; no one loses.

Jesus is talking about deferred gratification. The man who finds the treasure in the field pays a high price *now* by giving up all he has—but soon he'll gain a fabulous treasure. As long as his eyes are on that treasure, he makes his short-term sacrifices with joy. The joy is present, so the gratification isn't entirely deferred. Present joy comes from anticipating future joy.

What is this "treasure in heaven"? It includes power (Luke 19:15–19), possessions (Matthew 19:21), and pleasures (Psalm 16:11). Jesus promises that those who sacrifice on earth will receive "a hundred times as much" in heaven (Matthew 19:29). That's 10,000 percent—an impressive return!

Of course, Christ Himself is our ultimate treasure. All else pales in comparison to Him and the joy of knowing Him (Philippians 3:7–11). A person, Jesus, is our first treasure. A place, heaven, is our second treasure. Possessions, eternal rewards, are our third treasure. (What person are you living for? What place are you living for? What possessions are you living for?)

"Store up for yourselves treasures in heaven." Why? Because it's right? Not just that, but because it's *smart*. Because such treasures will *last*. Jesus argues from the bottom line. It's not an emotional appeal; it's a logical one: Invest in what has lasting value.

You'll never see a hearse pulling a U-Haul. Why? *Because you can't take it with you.*

> Do not be overawed when a man grows rich,
> > when the splendor of his house increases;
> for he will take nothing with him when he dies,
> > his splendor will not descend with him.
> (Psalm 49:16–17)

John D. Rockefeller was one of the wealthiest men who ever lived. After he died someone asked his accountant,

"How much money did John D. leave?" The reply was classic: "He left...*all* of it."

You can't take it with you.

If that point is clear in your mind, you're ready to hear the secret of the Treasure Principle.

THE TREASURE PRINCIPLE

Jesus takes that profound truth "You can't take it with you" and adds a stunning qualification. By telling us to store up treasures for ourselves in heaven, He gives us a breathtaking corollary, which I call the Treasure Principle:

> **You can't take it with you—
> but you *can* send it on ahead.**

It's that simple. And if it *doesn't* take your breath away, you're not understanding it! Anything we try to hang on to here will be lost. But anything we put into God's hands will be ours for eternity (insured for infinitely more than $100,000 by the real FDIC, the Father's Deposit Insurance Corporation).

If we give instead of keep, if we invest in the eternal instead of in the temporal, we store up treasures in heaven that will never stop paying dividends. Whatever treasures we store up on earth will be left behind when we leave.

Whatever treasures we store up in heaven will be waiting for us when we arrive.

Financial planners tell us, "When it comes to your money, don't think just three months or three years ahead. Think thirty years ahead." Christ, the ultimate investment counselor, takes it further. He says, "Don't ask how your investment will be paying off in just thirty years. Ask how it will be paying off in thirty *million* years."

Suppose I offer you one thousand dollars today to spend however you want. Not a bad deal. But suppose I give you a choice—you can either have that one thousand dollars today *or* you can have ten million dollars one year from now, then ten million more every year after that. Only a fool would take the thousand dollars today. Yet that's what we do whenever we grab onto something that will last for only a moment, forgoing something far more valuable that we could enjoy later for much longer.

Of course, there are many good things God wants us to do with money that don't involve giving it away. It is essential, for instance, that we provide for our family's basic material needs (1 Timothy 5:8). But these good things are only a beginning. The money God entrusts to us here on earth is eternal investment capital. Every day is an opportunity to buy up more shares in His kingdom.

You can't take it with you, but you can send it on ahead.

It's a revolutionary concept. If you embrace it, I guarantee it will change your life. As you store up heavenly treasures, you'll gain an everlasting version of what that man found in the treasure hidden in the field.

Joy.

Chapter 2

COMPOUNDING JOY

The less I spent on myself and the more I gave to others, the fuller of happiness and blessing did my soul become.

HUDSON TAYLOR

In 1990, I was a pastor of a large church, making a good salary and earning book royalties. I had been a pastor for thirteen years, since the church began. I didn't want to do anything else.

Then something happened that turned my family members' lives upside down. I was on the board of a crisis pregnancy center, and we had opened our home to a pregnant teenager, helping her give up her baby for adoption. We also had the joy of seeing her come to Christ.

I felt an even greater burden for the unborn. After searching Scripture and much prayer, I began participating in peaceful, nonviolent rescues at abortion clinics. For this I was arrested and sent to jail. An abortion clinic won a court judgment against a group of us. I told a judge that I would pay anything I owed, but I couldn't hand over money to people who would use it to kill babies. (This was a matter of conscience. Understand that I have never failed to pay other debts, nor do I recommend that others avoid paying them.)

Then I discovered that my church was about to receive a writ of garnishment demanding that they surrender one-fourth of my wages each month to the abortion clinic. The church would have to either pay the abortion clinic or defy a court order. To prevent this from happening, I resigned.

That judgment was one of the best things that ever happened to us.

I'd already divested myself of book royalties. The only way I could avoid garnishment was to make no more than minimum wage. Fortunately, our family had been living on only a portion of my church salary, and we had just made our final house payment, so we were out of debt.

Another court judgment followed, involving another abortion clinic. Though our actions had been nonviolent, the clinic was awarded the largest judgment ever against a group of peaceful protestors: $8.2 million. This time it seemed likely we would lose our house. By all appearances, and certainly by the world's standards, our lives had taken a devastating turn. Right?

Wrong. It was one of the best things that ever happened to us.

What others intended for evil, God intended for good (Genesis 50:20). We began a new ministry. My wife, Nanci, worked at a secretary's salary, supplementing my minimum wage. Her name alone was on all of our assets, including the house. My inability to legally own assets was nothing I sought after and nothing to be congratulated for, but God used it to help me understand what He means by "Everything under heaven belongs to me" (Job 41:11).

This wasn't the first time God taught me about His ownership. Many years ago, I loaned a new portable stereo to our church's high school group. It came back beat-up and, I admit, it bothered me. But the Lord convicted me, reminding me it wasn't *my* stereo—it was His. And it had been used to help reach young people. Who was I to complain about what was God's?

Back then the material possessions I valued most were my books. My money went toward many great books. Thousands of them. Those books meant a lot to me. I loaned them out, but it troubled me when they weren't returned or came back looking shabby.

Then I sensed God's leading to hand over the books—all of them—to begin a church library. I looked at the names of those who checked them out, sometimes dozens of names per book. I realized that by releasing the books, I had invested in others' lives. Suddenly, the more worn the book, the better. My perspective totally changed.

Fast-forwarding to the early 1990s, God used those court judgments to take my understanding of His ownership to a new level. Scripture really hit home:

- The earth is the LORD's, and everything in it, the world, and all who live in it. (Psalm 24:1)
- "The silver is mine and the gold is mine," declares the LORD Almighty. (Haggai 2:8)
- Remember the LORD your God, for it is he who gives you the ability to produce wealth. (Deuteronomy 8:18)
- You are not your own; you were bought at a price. (1 Corinthians 6:19–20)

God was teaching me the first of six keys to understanding the Treasure Principle:

God was and is the owner of everything, including books and stereos. He even owns me. God never revoked His ownership, never surrendered His claim to all treasures. He didn't die and leave the earth to me or anyone else.

TREASURE PRINCIPLE KEY #1

God owns everything.
I'm His money manager.

Ironically, I'd written extensively about God's owner-ship in my book *Money, Possessions and Eternity*. Within a year of its publication, I no longer owned anything. God was teaching me, in the crucible of adversity, the life-changing implications of that truth.

I realized that our house belonged to God, not us. Why worry about whether or not we would keep it if it belonged to Him anyway? He has no shortage of resources. He could easily provide us another place to live.

But understanding ownership was only half of my les-son. If God was the owner, I was the manager. I needed to adopt a steward's mentality toward the assets He had *entrusted*—not *given*—to me.

A steward manages assets for the owner's benefit. The steward carries no sense of entitlement to the assets he man-ages. It's his job to find out what the owner wants done with his assets, then carry out his will.

JOYFUL GIVING

Jerry Caven had a successful restaurant chain, two banks, a ranch, a farm, and real estate ventures. Now, at age fifty-nine, Jerry was searching for a nice lakeside retirement home. But the Owner had other plans.

"God led us to put our money and time overseas," Jerry says. "It's been exciting. Before, we gave token amounts. Now we put substantial money into missions. We often go to India."

What changed the Cavens' attitude toward giving?

"It was realizing God's ownership," Jerry explains. "Once we understood that we were giving away God's money to do God's work, we discovered a peace and joy we never had back when we thought it was our money!"

Once, a distraught man rode his horse up to John Wesley, shouting, "Mr. Wesley, something terrible happened! Your house burned to the ground!"

Wesley weighed the news, then calmly replied, "No. The *Lord's* house burned to the ground. That means one less responsibility for me."

Wesley's reaction wasn't denial. Rather, it was a bold affirmation of reality—God is the owner of all things, and we are simply His stewards.

Whenever we think like owners, it's a red flag. We should be thinking like stewards, investment managers, always looking for the best place to invest the Owner's money. At the end of our term of service, we'll undergo a job performance evaluation: "For we will all stand before God's judgment seat.... So then, each of us will give an account of himself to God" (Romans 14:10, 12).

Our name is on God's account. We have unrestricted access to it, a privilege that is subject to abuse. As His money managers, God trusts us to set our own salaries. We draw needed funds from His wealth to pay our living expenses. One of our central spiritual decisions is determining what is a reasonable amount to live on. Whatever that amount is—and it will legitimately vary from person to person—we shouldn't hoard or spend the excess. After all, it's His, not ours. And He has something to say about where to put it.

Every spring my wife and I read through dozens of letters from people in our church who are going on summer missions trips. This year we received forty-five requests asking us to pray and contribute financially. When this time comes each year, I'm like a kid in a candy store—a candy store as big as the world, as big as the heart of God.

Why such excitement?

Because we get to hear the stories and read the e-mails. We see the enthusiasm, the growth, the kingdom-mindedness, the changed priorities. We gain vested interest in more facets of God's work around the world. We pray that those who go—as well as those to whom they go—will never be the same. And we will have had a part in it!

Recently I was attending a gathering of givers. We went around the room and told our stories. The words *fun, joy, exciting,* and *wonderful* kept surfacing. There were lots of smiles and laughter, along with tears of joy. One older couple eagerly shared how they are always traveling around the world, getting involved in the ministries they're giving to. Meanwhile, their home in the states is becoming run-down. They said, "Our children keep telling us, 'Fix up your house or buy a new one. You can afford it.' We tell them, 'Why would we do that? That's not what excites us!'"

Ray Berryman, CEO for a national municipal services firm, says he and his wife give at least half of their income to God's work each year.

"My joy in giving comes from serving God in a way that I know He's called me to and realizing that what I give is impacting people for Christ," Ray says. "It's exciting to know we're part of evangelizing, discipling, helping, and feeding the needy. It just feels wonderful and fulfilling."

The more we give, the more we delight in our giving—and the more God delights in us. Our giving pleases us. But more importantly, it pleases God.

"God loves a cheerful giver" (2 Corinthians 9:7). This doesn't mean we should give only when we're feeling cheerful. The cheerfulness often comes during and after the act of obedience, not before it. So don't wait until you feel like giving—

it could be a long wait! Just give and watch the joy follow.

God delights in our cheerfulness in giving. He wants us to find joy. He even *commands* us to rejoice (Philippians 4:4). What command could be a greater pleasure to obey than that one? But if we don't give, we're robbed of the source of joy God instructs us to seek!

I know a single man who came to Christ in his twenties, read the Scriptures, and got so excited that he decided to sell his house and give the money to God. But when he shared this plan with older believers in his Bible-study group, something tragic happened: They talked him out of it.

If you ever feel inclined to talk a young believer (including your own child) out of giving, restrain yourself. Don't quench the Spirit of God, and don't rob someone of the present joy and future rewards of giving. Instead, watch and learn. Then lay God's assets on the table, and ask Him what He wants you to give away.

> *Giving isn't a luxury of the rich. It's a privilege of the poor.*

THUNDER, LIGHTNING, AND GRACE

The Macedonian Christians understood the joy of giving: "Out of the most severe trial, their overflowing joy and their extreme poverty welled up in rich generosity" (2 Corinthians 8:2).

How do "severe trial," "overflowing joy," "extreme poverty," and "rich generosity" all fit together in one verse? Giving isn't a luxury of the rich. It's a privilege of the poor. I've discovered that impoverished Christians find no greater joy than in giving.

The Macedonians refused to let hard circumstances keep them from joy: "They urgently pleaded with us for the privilege of sharing in this service to the saints" (v. 4). They had to plead, presumably because Paul and others were telling them that their poverty exempted them from giving.

These early Christians were dirt-poor but came up with every reason they could to give. They begged for the privilege of giving! What a contrast to us, who have so much more than they had but manage to come up with endless justifications for *not* giving!

It's humbling to receive gifts from people in far greater need than you. I've experienced this on missions trips where the poor serve their very best food to visiting Americans and do it with great smiles of joy. They're not pretending that this sacrifice makes them happy. It *really* does.

When the tabernacle was being built, people were so caught up in the excitement they had to be "restrained" from giving more (Exodus 36:5–7). That's what giving will do to you.

David looked at what he and his people were giving to the Lord. It humbled him: "But who am I, and who are my people, that we should be able to give as generously as this? Everything comes from you, and we have given you only what comes from your hand" (1 Chronicles 29:14).

My friend Dixie Fraley told me, "We're most like God when we're giving." Gaze upon Christ long enough, and you'll become more of a giver. Give long enough, and you'll become more like Christ.

Paul says in 2 Corinthians 8:1: "We want you to know about the grace that God has given the Macedonian churches." How was God's grace demonstrated? By their act of giving to needy Christians. In verse 6, Paul calls the Macedonians' giving to help the hungry in Jerusalem an "act of grace." The same Greek word is used for Christian *giving* as for God's *grace*.

Christ's grace defines, motivates, and puts in perspective our giving: "For you know the grace of our Lord Jesus Christ, that though he was rich, yet for your sakes he became poor, so that you through his poverty might become rich" (v. 9).

Our giving is a reflexive response to the grace of God in our lives. It doesn't come out of our altruism or philanthropy—it comes out of the transforming work of Christ in us. This grace is the action; our giving is the reaction. We give because He first gave to us. The greatest passage on giving in all Scripture ends not with "Congratulations for your generosity," but "Thanks be to God for his indescribable gift!" (2 Corinthians 9:15).

As thunder follows lightning, giving follows grace. When God's grace touches you, you can't help but respond with generous giving. And as the Macedonians knew, giving is simply the overflow of joy.

THE FRINGE BENEFITS OF GIVING

Mark, a Kentucky attorney, gives away half of his income each year.

"My pursuit of money drove me away from God," Mark says. "But since I've been giving it to Him, everything's changed. In fact, giving has brought me closer to God than anything else."

In the movie *Chariots of Fire*, Olympian Eric Liddell said, "I believe God made me for a purpose...and when I run, I feel His pleasure." Those who've discovered the Treasure Principle will testify, "When I give, I feel His pleasure."

There have been days when I've lost focus, and then a need arises and God leads me to give. Suddenly I'm infused with energy, purpose, and joy. I feel God's pleasure.

God said, "I give to the Levites as their inheritance the

tithes that the Israelites present as an offering to the LORD"
(Numbers 18:24). Notice that the people gave their money
to God, not the Levites. It may have looked like the people
were giving to their spiritual leaders, but they actually gave
to God, and it was He who then designated His funds to
the Levites. Christians should love their pastors and support
them financially (Galatians 6:6), but first and foremost we
give to God (2 Corinthians 8:5). Before anything else, giving is an act of worship.

Giving jump-starts our relationship with God. It opens
our fists so we can receive what God has for us. When we
see what it does for others and for us, we open our fists
sooner and wider when the next chance comes.

God says, "If a man shuts his ears to the cry of the poor,
he too will cry out and not be answered" (Proverbs 21:13).
In Isaiah 58:6–10, God says that His willingness to answer
our prayers is directly affected by whether we are caring for
the hungry, needy, and oppressed. Want to empower your
prayer life? Give.

It was said of Josiah, "He defended the cause of the
poor and needy, and so all went well. Is that not what it
means to know me?" declares the LORD (Jeremiah 22:16).
Caring for the needy flows out of knowing God, and draws
us closer to Him.

Businessman Hal Thomas told me, "When I give,

I'm saying, 'I love You, Lord.'" Paul told the Corinthians their financial gift was "overflowing in many expressions of thanks to God" (2 Corinthians 9:12).

Another benefit of giving is freedom. It's a matter of basic physics. The greater the mass, the greater the hold that mass exerts. The more things we own—the greater their total mass—the more they grip us, setting us in orbit around them. Finally, like a black hole, they suck us in.

Giving changes all that. It breaks us out of orbit around our possessions. We escape their gravity, entering a new orbit around our treasures in heaven.

Despite the $8.2 million court judgment eleven years ago, we never lost our house. While paying me a minimum-wage salary, the ministry owned the books I wrote. And suddenly royalties increased. Our ministry has been able to give away about 100 percent of those royalties to missions, famine relief, and pro-life work. Since EPM began, by God's grace, we've given over $5 million. Sometimes I think God sells the books just to raise funds for ministries close to His heart!

You couldn't pay me enough not to give.

I don't go to bed at night feeling that I've "sacrificed" that money. I go to bed feeling joy, because there's nothing like giving. For me, the only feeling that compares is the joy of leading someone to Christ.

Giving infuses life with joy. It interjects an eternal dimension into even the most ordinary day. That's just one reason you couldn't pay me enough not to give.

But hold on—great as it is, our present joy isn't the best part of the Treasure Principle.

Chapter 3

EYES ON ETERNITY

*"For the Son of Man is going to come in his
Father's glory with his angels, and then he will reward
each person according to what he has done."*

MATTHEW 16:27

The streets of Cairo were hot and dusty. Pat and Rakel
Thurman took us down an alley. We drove past Arabic
signs to a gate that opened to a plot of overgrown grass. It
was a graveyard for American missionaries.

As my family and I followed, Pat pointed to a sun-
scorched tombstone that read: "William Borden,
1887–1913."

Borden, a Yale graduate and heir to great wealth,
rejected a life of ease in order to bring the gospel to
Muslims. Refusing even to buy himself a car, Borden gave
away hundreds of thousands of dollars to missions. After

only four months of zealous ministry in Egypt, he contracted spinal meningitis and died at the age of twenty-five.

I dusted off the epitaph on Borden's grave. After describing his love and sacrifices for the kingdom of God and for Muslim people, the inscription ended with a phrase I've never forgotten: "Apart from faith in Christ, there is no explanation for such a life."

The Thurmans took us straight from Borden's grave to the Egyptian National Museum. The King Tut exhibit was mind-boggling.

Tutankhamen, the boy king, was only seventeen when he died. He was buried with solid gold chariots and thousands of golden artifacts. His gold coffin was found within gold tombs within gold tombs within gold tombs. The burial site was filled with *tons* of gold.

The Egyptians believed in an afterlife—one where they could take earthly treasures. But all the treasures intended for King Tut's eternal enjoyment stayed right where they were until Howard Carter discovered the burial chamber in 1922. They hadn't been touched for more than three thousand years.

I was struck by the contrast between these two graves. Borden's was obscure, dusty, and hidden off the back alley of a street littered with garbage. Tutankhamen's tomb glittered with unimaginable wealth. Yet where are these two young men now? One, who lived in opulence and called himself king, is in the misery of a Christless eternity. The other, who lived a modest life on earth in service of the one true King, is enjoying his everlasting reward in the presence of his Lord.

Tut's life was tragic because of an awful truth discovered too late—he couldn't take his treasures with him. William Borden's life was triumphant. Why? Because instead of leaving behind his treasures, he sent them on ahead.

ETERNAL REWARDS

If you imagine heaven as a place where you will strum a harp in endless tedium, you probably dread it. But if you trust Scripture, you will be filled with joy and excitement as you anticipate your heavenly home. As I've written elsewhere, heaven will be a place of rest and relief from the burdens of sin and suffering; but it will also be a place of great learning, activity, artistic expression, exploration, discovery, camaraderie, and service.[1]

Some of us will reign with Christ (Revelation 20:6). Faithful servants will be put "in charge of many things" (Matthew 25:21, 23). Christ will grant some followers leadership over cities, in proportion to their service on earth (Luke 19:12–19). Scripture refers to five different crowns, suggesting leadership positions. We'll even command angels (1 Corinthians 6:3).

We are given these eternal rewards for doing good works (Ephesians 6:8; Romans 2:6, 10), persevering under persecution (Luke 6:22–23), showing compassion to the needy (Luke 14:13–14), and treating our enemies kindly (Luke 6:35).

God also grants us rewards for generous giving: "Go, sell your possessions and give to the poor, and you will have treasure in heaven" (Matthew 19:21).

Jesus is keeping track of our smallest acts of kindness: "If anyone gives even a cup of cold water to one of these little ones because he is my disciple, I tell you the truth, he will certainly not lose his reward" (Matthew 10:42).

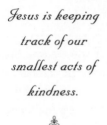

Jesus is keeping track of our smallest acts of kindness.

God is keeping a record of all we do for Him, including our giving: "A scroll of remembrance was written in his presence concerning those who feared the LORD and honored his name" (Malachi 3:16).

Imagine a scribe in heaven recording each of your gifts on that scroll. The bike you gave to the neighbor kid, the books to prisoners, the monthly checks to the church, missionaries, and pregnancy center—all are being chronicled. Scrolls are made to be read. I look forward to hearing your giving stories and meeting those touched by what you gave.

Jesus said, "If you have not been trustworthy in handling

worldly wealth, who will trust you with true riches? And if you have not been trustworthy with someone else's property, who will give you property of your own?" (Luke 16:11–12). If you handle His money faithfully, Christ will give you true riches—eternal ones.

By clinging to what isn't ours, we forgo the opportunity to be granted ownership in heaven. But by generously distributing God's property on earth, we will become property owners in heaven!

Many benefits of our present giving will come to us in heaven. After speaking of the shrewd servant's desire to use earthly resources so that "people will welcome me into their houses" (Luke 16:4), Jesus told His followers to use "worldly wealth" (earthly resources) to "gain friends" (by making a difference in their lives on earth). The reason? "So that when it is gone [when life on earth is over] you will be welcomed into eternal dwellings" (v. 9).

Our "friends" in heaven will be those whose lives we've touched on earth, who will have their own "eternal dwellings." Luke 16:9 seems to say our friends' eternal dwellings are places where we stay and fellowship, perhaps as we move about the heavenly kingdom. The money we give to help others on earth will open doors of fellowship with them in heaven. Now *that's* something to get excited about!

John Bunyan wrote *Pilgrim's Progress* in an English prison. He said:

Whatever good thing you do for Him, if done according to the Word, is laid up for you as treasure in chests and coffers, to be brought out to be rewarded before both men and angels, to your eternal comfort.[2]

Is this a biblical concept? Absolutely. Paul spoke about the Philippians' financial giving and explained, "Not that I am looking for a gift, but I am looking for what may be credited to your account" (Philippians 4:17). God keeps an account open for us in heaven, and every gift given for His glory is a deposit in that account. Not only God, not only others, but *we* are the eternal beneficiaries of our giving. (Have you been making regular deposits?)

But isn't it wrong to be motivated by reward? No, it isn't. If it were wrong, Christ wouldn't offer it to us as a motivation. Reward is His idea, not ours.

Our instinct is to give to those who will give us something in return. But Jesus told us to give to "the poor, the crippled, the lame, the blind.... Although they cannot repay you, you will be repaid at the resurrection of the righteous" (Luke 14:13–14). If we give to those who can't reward us, Christ guarantees He will personally reward us in heaven.

Giving is a giant lever positioned on the fulcrum of this world, allowing us to move mountains in the next world. Because we give, eternity will be different—for others and for us.

A HEART IN THE RIGHT PLACE

Ever hear the song "Thank You (for Giving to the Lord)"? It depicts us meeting people in heaven who explain how our giving changed their lives. Whether we were their Sunday school teacher or put money in the offering, these people will one day express their gratitude to us for our giving.

God promises us generous heavenly rewards, in a magnificent New Heaven and New Earth, no longer under the curse and no longer suffering (Revelation 21:1–6). We'll forever be with the person we were made for, in a place made for us.

> *Many Christians dread the thought of leaving this world.*

Nevertheless, many Christians dread the thought of leaving this world.

Why? Because so many have stored up their treasures on earth, not in heaven. Each day brings us closer to death. If your treasures are on earth, that means each day brings you closer to losing your treasures.

John Wesley toured a vast estate with a proud plantation owner. They rode their horses for hours and saw only a fraction of the man's property. At the end of the day they sat down to dinner. The plantation owner eagerly asked, "Well, Mr. Wesley, what do you think?"

Wesley replied, "I think you're going to have a hard time leaving all this."

I recently spoke with Laverne, a woman with terminal cancer. She was crying—not because she's going to die, but because I asked her to talk about giving. Through tears she said, "Giving melts me. It blows me away to know that God's chosen me to give. It won't be long before I see Him face-to-face. I just want to hear Him say, 'Well done, my good and faithful servant.'"

Suddenly, Laverne laughed. "I mean, what else matters?" she said. "Why should I care about anything else?"

Laverne's heart is focused on heavenly treasures. Because she is storing up treasures in heaven, each day brings her closer to those treasures.

Jesus said, "Where your treasure is, there your heart will be also" (Matthew 6:21). That's the second key to the Treasure Principle.

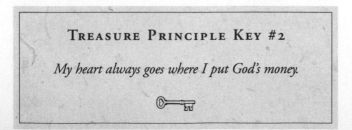

TREASURE PRINCIPLE KEY #2

My heart always goes where I put God's money.

By telling us that our hearts follow our treasure, Jesus is saying, "Show me your checkbook, your VISA statement, and your receipts, and I'll show you where your heart is."

Suppose you buy shares of General Motors. What happens? You suddenly develop interest in GM. You check the financial pages. You see a magazine article about GM and read every word, even though a month ago you would have passed right over it.

Suppose you're giving to help African children with AIDS. When you see an article on the subject, you're hooked. If you're sending money to plant churches in India and an earthquake hits India, you watch the news and fervently pray.

As surely as the compass needle follows north, your heart will follow your treasure. Money leads; hearts follow.

As surely as the compass needle follows north, your heart will follow your treasure.

I've heard people say, "I want more of a heart for missions." I always respond, "Jesus tells you exactly how to get it. Put your money in missions—and in your church and the poor—and your heart will follow."

Do you wish you cared more about eternal things? Then reallocate some of your money, maybe *most* of your money, from temporal things to eternal things. Watch what happens.

God wants your heart. He isn't looking just for "donors" for His kingdom, those who stand outside the cause and dispassionately consider acts of philanthropy. He's looking for disciples immersed in the causes they give to. He wants people so filled with a vision for eternity that they wouldn't dream of not investing their money, time, and prayers where they will matter most.

Of course, giving isn't the only good thing we can do with money. We need to feed, clothe, house, and transport our families. But when the basics are taken care of, why shouldn't the rest go toward treasures in heaven?

Moses left Egypt's treasures "because he was looking ahead to his reward" (Hebrews 11:26).

He who lays up treasures on earth spends his life backing away from his treasures. To him, death is loss.

He who lays up treasures in heaven looks forward to eternity; he's moving daily toward his treasures. To him, death is gain.

He who spends his life moving away from his treasures has reason to despair. He who spends his life moving toward his treasures has reason to rejoice.

Are you despairing or rejoicing?

Chapter 4

ROADBLOCKS
TO GIVING

*"Be on your guard against all kinds of greed; a man's life
does not consist in the abundance of his possessions."*

LUKE 12:15

We know that Christ commands us to give. And we know He
offers us great rewards for giving. So why is it so hard to give?

There are many roadblocks to giving: unbelief, insecurity, pride, idolatry, desire for power and control. The raging
current of our culture—and often our churches—makes it
hard to swim upstream. It's considered "normal" to keep far
more than we give.

But I'm convinced that the greatest deterrent to giving
is this: the illusion that earth is our home. This leads us to
the next key to the Treasure Principle:

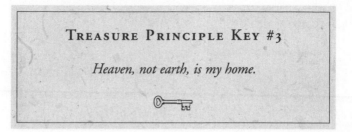

TREASURE PRINCIPLE KEY #3

Heaven, not earth, is my home.

The Bible says we're pilgrims, strangers, aliens on earth (Hebrews 11:13). We're ambassadors representing our true country (2 Corinthians 5:20). "Our citizenship is in heaven" (Philippians 3:20). We're citizens of "a better country—a heavenly one" (Hebrews 11:16).

Where we choose to store our treasures depends largely on where we think our home is.

Suppose your home is in France and you're visiting America for three months, living in a hotel. You're told that you can't bring anything back to France on your flight home. But you can earn money and mail deposits to your bank in France.

Would you fill your hotel room with expensive furniture and wall hangings? Of course not. You'd send your money where your home is. You would spend only what you needed on the temporary residence, sending your treasures ahead so they'd be waiting for you when you got home.

Both of our daughters got married recently. Friends and family set aside their busy schedules and traveled in from all over the country. When the King's wedding day comes, the universe will screech to a halt (Revelation 19:7–9). Nothing else will be on heaven's calendar. The Groom from Nazareth and His beloved bride will take center stage.

Every day of our lives we're traveling toward that wedding—*our* wedding! It's closer today than it was yesterday.

Our home is a place we've never been.

Our Bridegroom, the Carpenter, is building a place for us in heaven. Everything we send on ahead will be waiting there for us. It's our gift to Him, but in His generosity He will give those treasures back to us.

Jesus is a builder by trade. He's also omniscient and omnipotent, qualities that come in handy on a building project! Don't you think that the home He's been building for us the last two thousand years is something incredible?

Paradoxically, our home is a place we've never been. But it's the place we were made for, the place made for us.

If we would let this reality sink in, it would forever change the way we think and live. We would stop laying up treasures in our earthly hotel rooms and start sending more ahead to our true home.

THE MOST TOYS

Take a ride with me. After a few miles we turn off the road, pass through a gate, and fall in line behind some pickup trucks. The vehicles ahead are filled with computers, stereo systems, furniture, appliances, fishing gear, and toys.

Higher and higher we climb, until we reach a parking lot. There the drivers unload their cargo. Curious, you watch a man hoist a computer. He staggers to the corner of the lot, then hurls his computer over the edge.

The man hurls his computer over the edge.

Now you've got to find out what's going on. You scramble out of the car and peer over the precipice. At the bottom of the cliff is a giant pit filled with…stuff.

Finally you understand. This is a landfill, a junkyard the final resting place for the things in our lives.

Sooner or later, everything we own ends up here. Christmas and birthday presents. Cars, boats, and hot tubs. Clothes, stereos, and barbecues. The treasures that children quarreled about, friendships were lost over, honesty was sacrificed for, and marriages broke up over—all end up here. (I recommend taking a family field trip to a junkyard. It's a powerful object lesson.)

Ever seen that bumper sticker "He who dies with the most toys wins"? Millions of people act as if it were true. The more accurate saying is "He who dies with the most toys still dies—and never takes his toys with him." When we die after devoting our lives to acquiring things, we don't win—we lose. We move into eternity, but our toys stay behind, filling junkyards. The bumper sticker couldn't be more wrong.

I think of it in terms of a dot and a line. Our lives have two phases: one a dot, the other a line extending out from that dot.

Our present life on earth is the dot. It begins. It ends. It's brief. But from that dot extends a line that goes on forever. That line is eternity, which Christians will spend in heaven.

The Dot: The Line:

Life on earth   Life in heaven

Right now we're living *in* the dot. But what are we living *for*? The shortsighted person lives for the dot. The person with perspective lives for the line.

This earth (and my time here) is the dot. My beloved Bridegroom, the coming wedding, the Great Reunion, and my eternal home in the New Heaven and New Earth—they're all on the line. That's our next key:

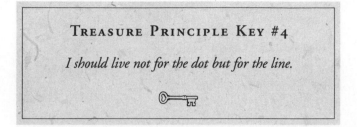

TREASURE PRINCIPLE KEY #4

I should live not for the dot but for the line.

The person who lives for the dot lives for treasures on earth that end up in junkyards. The person who lives for the line lives for treasures in heaven that will never end.

Giving is living for the line.

We'll each part with our money. The only question is when. We have no choice but to part with it later. But we do have a choice whether to part with it *now*. We can keep earthly treasures for the moment, and we may derive some temporary enjoyment from them. But if we give them away, we'll enjoy eternal treasures that will never be taken from us.

This is what Jim Elliot was talking about when he said, "He is no fool who gives what he cannot keep to gain what he cannot lose." If you hear those words and think, *Oh, he was one of those superspiritual missionary types who didn't think about gain,* then you missed the whole point. Read it again. Gain was *precisely* what Jim Elliot was thinking about! He just wanted the kind of gain he couldn't lose. He wanted his treasures in heaven.

Live for the line, not for the dot.

POSSESSION OBSESSION

A PBS television program called *Affluenza* addresses what it calls the "modern-day plague of materialism." The program claims:

- The average American shops six hours a week while spending forty minutes playing with his children.
- By age twenty, we've seen one million commercials.
- Recently, more Americans declared bankruptcy than graduated from college.
- In 90 percent of divorce cases, arguments about money play a prominent role.

What strikes me about this program is that it doesn't argue against materialism on a moral basis but a pragmatic one: Material wealth doesn't make us happy.

Listen to some of the wealthiest people of their day:

- "The care of $200 million is enough to kill anyone. There is no pleasure in it." W. H. VANDERBILT
- "I am the most miserable man on earth." JOHN JACOB ASTOR
- "I have made many millions, but they have brought me no happiness." JOHN D. ROCKEFELLER
- "Millionaires seldom smile." ANDREW CARNEGIE

- "I was happier when doing a mechanic's job." HENRY FORD

You've read the stories of lottery winners who are more miserable a few years after winning than they were before. The wealth they dreamed would bring them happiness didn't. Not even close.

At the airport, Hugh Maclellan Jr. saw an acquaintance who looked troubled.

"What's the matter?" Hugh asked.

The man sighed. "I thought I was finally going to have a weekend to myself. But now I have to go supervise repairs on my house in Florida." Dejected, he sat waiting to take off in his private jet.

We think we own our possessions, but too often they own us.

Here's a man with everything he needs, with what most people dream of; yet he couldn't even enjoy his weekend. He was enslaved by his possessions. We think we own our possessions, but too often they own us.

Nothing makes a journey more difficult than a heavy backpack filled with nice but unnecessary things. Pilgrims travel light.

THE TYRANNY OF THINGS

Nanci and I have lived in our house for twenty-three years. For the first nine years we had ugly, orange carpet. We never cared what happened to it. The day we finally installed a new carpet, someone lit a candle. The match head fell off and burned a hole in the carpet.

The day before we wouldn't have cared. Now we were upset. Were we better off with our nice new possession?

Every item we buy is one more thing to think about, talk about, clean, repair, rearrange, fret over, and replace when it goes bad.

Let's say I get a television for free. Now what? I hook up the antenna or subscribe to a cable service. I buy a new VCR or DVD player. I rent movies. I get surround-sound speakers. I buy a recliner so I can watch my programs in comfort. This all costs money. But it also takes large amounts of time, energy, and attention.

The time I devote to my TV and its accessories means less time for communicating with my family, reading the Word, praying, opening our home, or ministering to the needy.

So what's the true cost of my "free" television?

Acquiring a possession may push me into redefining my priorities. If I buy a boat, I'll want to justify my purchase by *using* the boat, which may mean frequent week-ends away from my family or church, making me unavailable to attend my daughter's basketball game or teach a Sunday school class or work in the nursery.

The problem isn't the boat or the television. The problem is me. It's a law of life, the tyranny of things.

CHASING THE WIND

Solomon makes a series of insightful statements in Ecclesiastes 5:10–15. I'll follow each with my paraphrase:

- "Whoever loves money never has money enough" (v. 10). *The more you have, the more you want.*
- "Whoever loves wealth is never satisfied with his income" (v. 10). *The more you have, the less you're satisfied.*
- "As goods increase, so do those who consume them" (v. 11). *The more you have, the more people (including the government) will come after it.*
- "And what benefit are they to the owner except to feast his eyes on them?" (v. 11). *The more you have, the more you realize it does you no good.*
- "The sleep of a laborer is sweet, whether he eats little or much, but the abundance of a rich man permits him no sleep" (v. 12). *The more you have, the more you have to worry about.*

- "I have seen a grievous evil under the sun: wealth hoarded to the harm of its owner" (v. 13). *The more you have, the more you can hurt yourself by holding on to it.*
- "Or wealth lost through some misfortune" (v.14). *The more you have, the more you have to lose.*
- "Naked a man comes from his mother's womb, and as he comes, so he departs. He takes nothing from his labor that he can carry in his hand" (v. 15). *The more you have, the more you'll leave behind.*

As the wealthiest man on earth, Solomon learned that affluence didn't satisfy. All it did was give him greater opportunity to chase more mirages. People tend to run out of money before mirages, so they cling to the myth that things they can't afford will satisfy them. Solomon's money never ran out. He tried everything, saying, "I denied myself nothing my eyes desired; I refused my heart no pleasure" (Ecclesiastes 2:10).

Solomon's conclusion? "When I surveyed all that my hands had done and what I had toiled to achieve, everything was meaningless, a chasing after the wind; nothing was gained under the sun" (v. 11).

Why do we keep getting fooled? Because our hearts yearn for treasure here and now. We're tempted to imagine that the earthly treasures we see around us are the genuine items rather than mere shadows of the real treasures.

But earthly treasures can become heavenly ones. A. W. Tozer said:

> As base a thing as money often is, it yet can be transmuted into everlasting treasure. It can be converted into food for the hungry and clothing for the poor; it can keep a missionary actively winning lost men to the light of the gospel and thus transmute itself into heavenly values. Any temporal possession can be turned into everlasting wealth. Whatever is given to Christ is immediately touched with immortality.[3]

If affluenza is the disease, what's the cure? If materialism is the poison, what's the antidote? Paul offers an answer:

> Command those who are rich in this present world not to be arrogant nor to put their hope in wealth, which is so uncertain, but to put their hope in God, who richly provides us with everything for our enjoyment. Command them to do good, to be rich in good deeds, and to be generous and willing to share. In this way they will lay up treasure for themselves as a firm foundation for the coming age, so that they may take hold of the life that is truly life. (1 Timothy 6:17–19)

Notice how Paul brings us right back to the Treasure Principle. When he speaks of giving to "lay up treasure for themselves as a firm foundation for the coming age," he's no doubt thinking directly of Christ's words in Matthew 6.

I carry in my wallet a little card. On one side it says, "God owns it all. I'm His money manager." Near this are three Scriptures. The other side says, "God cares what I do with the money He entrusts to me (I better ask Him)." Near this are Christ's words in Matthew 6 and Paul's in 2 Corinthians. Keeping the card near my cash is a powerful reminder of what is true.[4]

Paul says that being "generous" and "willing to share" and being "rich in good deeds" allows us to "take hold of the life that is truly life." As opposed to what? The second-class, so-called "life" of materialism.

That leads us to the fifth key to the Treasure Principle:

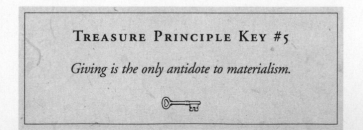

TREASURE PRINCIPLE KEY #5

Giving is the only antidote to materialism.

The act of giving is a vivid reminder that it's all about God, not about us. It's saying I am not the point, *He* is the point. He does not exist for me. I exist for Him. God's money has a higher purpose than my affluence. Giving is a joyful surrender to a greater person and a greater agenda. Giving affirms Christ's lordship. It dethrones me and exalts Him. It breaks the chains of mammon that would enslave me.

As long as I still have something, I believe I own it. But when I give it away, I relinquish control, power, and prestige. At the moment of release the light turns on. The magic spell is broken. My mind clears. I recognize God as owner, myself as servant, and others as intended beneficiaries of what God has entrusted to me.

Giving doesn't strip me of vested interests; rather, it shifts my vested interests from earth to heaven—from self to God.

Of course, money isn't all I can give. Time, wisdom, and expertise are wonderful gifts. Giving in any form breaks affluenza's fever. Giving breaks me free from the gravitational hold of money and possessions. Giving shifts me to a new center of gravity—heaven.

MUD PIES IN THE SLUM

After exposing the Laodiceans' spiritual poverty hidden beneath their wealth, Jesus offered them real treasures: "I counsel you to buy from me gold refined in the fire, so you can become rich" (Revelation 3:18).

When Christ returns, the world "will be destroyed by fire, and the earth and everything in it will be laid bare" (2 Peter 3:10). Does that sound depressing? It *would* be depressing if this world were our home. But it isn't! It *would* be depressing if we couldn't use our lives and resources to make a difference for eternity. But we can!

C. S. Lewis put it this way:

> We are halfhearted creatures, fooling about with drink and sex and ambition when infinite joy is offered us, like an ignorant child who wants to go on making mud pies in a slum because he cannot imagine what is meant by the offer of a holiday at sea. We are far too easily pleased. [5]

Even many Christians have settled for a life of unsatisfying material acquisitions, like making mud pies in a slum.

There's something so much better than anything the world can offer—eternal treasures and exhilarating joy.

You want these treasures and this joy, don't you? But maybe you have some practical questions about giving, or you're not sure where to start.

Keep reading.

Chapter 5

GETTING STARTED

I have held many things in my hands and I have lost them all.
But whatever I have placed in God's hands, that I still possess.

MARTIN LUTHER

To everyone's amazement, Sam Houston, the colorful soldier and politician, came to Christ. After his baptism, Houston said he wanted to pay half the local minister's salary. When someone asked him why, he responded, "My pocketbook was baptized, too."

Like Sam Houston, you may understand that the Christian life is inseparable from giving. But you might be wondering, *Where do I start?*

A logical place is where God started His Old Covenant children: "A tithe of everything from the land, whether grain from the soil or fruit from the trees, belongs to the LORD; it is holy to the LORD" (Leviticus 27:30).

The meaning of the word *tithe* is "a tenth part." Ten percent was to be given back to God. There were freewill offerings, too, but the 10 percent was mandatory.

Proverbs 3:9 says, "Honor the LORD with your wealth, with the *firstfruits* of all your crops" (emphasis mine). God's children give to Him first, not last.

When His children weren't giving as they should, He said, "Will a man rob God? Yet you rob me. But you ask, 'How do we rob you?' In tithes and offerings. You are under a curse—the whole nation of you—because you are robbing me. Bring the whole tithe into the storehouse, that there may be food in my house" (Malachi 3:8–10).

Jesus validated the mandatory tithe, even on small things (Matthew 23:23). But there's no mention of tithing after the Gospels. Other than the Hebrews 7:2–9 reference to Abraham tithing to Melchizedek, which isn't about the practice of the New Testament church. It's neither commanded nor rescinded, and there's heated debate among Christians about whether tithing is still a starting place for giving.

I have mixed feelings on this issue. I detest legalism. I certainly don't want to try to pour new wine into old wineskins, imposing superseded First Covenant restrictions on Christians. Every New Testament example of giving goes far beyond the tithe. However, none falls short of it.

There's a timeless truth behind the concept of giving God our firstfruits. Whether or not the tithe is still the minimal measure of those firstfruits, I ask myself, *Does God expect His New Covenant children to give less or more?* Jesus raised the spiritual bar; He never lowered it (Matthew 5:27–28).

TRAINING WHEELS

Maybe you believe exclusively in "grace giving" and disagree with the church fathers Origen, Jerome, and Augustine, who taught that the tithe was the minimum giving requirement for Christians. But it seems fair to ask, "God, do You really expect less of me—who has Your Holy Spirit within and lives in the wealthiest society in human history—than You demanded of the poorest Israelite?"

Nearly every study indicates that American Christians give on average between 2 and 3 percent of their income. A 2001 Barna Research report states:

> Among born again adults, there was a 44 percent rise in those who gave nothing last year. Compared to 1999, the mean per capita donation to churches dropped by 19 percent in 2000. One-third of born again adults said they tithed in 2000, but a comparison of their actual giving and household incomes reveals that only one-eighth did so. [6]

Isn't it troubling that in this wealthy society, "grace giving" amounts to a small fraction of the First Covenant standard? Whatever we're teaching about giving today, either it's not true to Scripture, the message isn't getting through, or we're being disobedient.

The tithe is God's historical method to get us on the path of giving. In that sense, it can serve as a gateway to the joy of grace giving. It's unhealthy to view tithing as a place to stop, but it can still be a good place to start. (Even under the First Covenant it wasn't a stopping place—don't forget the freewill offerings.)

Tithing isn't the ceiling of giving; it's the floor. It's not the finish line of giving; it's just the starting blocks. Tithes can be the training wheels to launch us into the mind-set, skills, and habits of grace giving.

Malachi says that the Israelites robbed God by withholding not only their mandatory tithes but also their voluntary "offerings." By giving less in their freewill offerings than He expected of them, they were robbing God. If they could rob God with insufficient freewill offerings, can't we do the same today?

Paul encouraged voluntary giving, yet also described such giving as "obedience" (2 Corinthians 9:13). God has expectations of us, even when our offerings are voluntary. To give less than He expects of us is to rob Him.

Of course, God doesn't expect us all to give the same

amount. We're to give in proportion to how He's blessed us (Deuteronomy 16:10, 16–17).

Some say, "We'll take this gradually. We're starting with 5 percent." But that's like saying, "I used to rob six convenience stores a year. This year, by His grace, I'm going to rob only three."

The point is not to rob God *less*—it's not to rob God *at all*.

> "I used to rob six convenience stores a year. This year, by His grace, I'm going to rob only three."

True, some would be sacrificing more by giving 5 percent of their income than others would be by tithing or even giving 50 or 90 percent. Certainly the affluent should never "check off the box," as if giving 10 percent automati-cally fulfills their obligation. The 90 percent belongs to God, too. He doesn't look at just what we give. He also looks at what we keep.

I've had the privilege of interviewing many givers. In the great majority of cases they mention tithing as the practice that first stretched them to give more. They tithed and then watched God provide. They saw their hearts move deeper into His kingdom. Now, years later, they're giving 60, 80, or even 95 percent of their incomes! But it was tithing that set them on the road to giving.

When God's people were robbing Him by withholding tithes and offerings, He said, "Test me in this…and see if I will not throw open the floodgates of heaven and pour out so much blessing that you will not have room enough for it" (Malachi 3:10).

Ironically, many people can't afford to give precisely *because* they're not giving (Haggai 1:9–11). If we pay our debt to God first, then we will incur His blessing to help us pay our debts to men. But when we rob God to pay men, we rob ourselves of God's blessing. No wonder we don't have enough. It's a vicious cycle, and it takes obedient faith to break out of it.

When people tell me they can't afford to tithe, I ask them, "If your income was reduced by 10 percent would you die?" They say, "No." And I say, "Then you've admitted that you can afford to tithe. It's just that you don't *want* to."

I'm not saying that it's easy to give. I'm saying—and there are thousands who will agree—that it's much easier to live on 90 percent or 50 percent or 10 percent of your income *inside* the will of God than it is to live on 100 percent *outside* it.

Tithing is like a toddler's first steps: They aren't his last or best steps, but they're a good start. Once you learn to ride a bike, you don't need the training wheels. Once you learn to give, tithing becomes irrelevant. And if you can ride the bike without ever using training wheels, good for you.

I have no problem with people who say "we're not

under the tithe," just as long as they're not using that as justification for giving less. But in my mind the current giving statistics among Christians clearly indicate most of us need a giving jump-start. If you find a gateway to giving that's better than the tithe, wonderful. But if not, why not start where God started His First Covenant children?

EXCELLENT GIVING

Paul said, "See that you also excel in this grace of giving" (2 Corinthians 8:7). Like piano playing, giving is a skill. With practice, we get better at it. We can learn to give more, give more often, and give more strategically. We teach the pursuit of excellence in our vocations. Why not make giving something we study, discuss, and sharpen, striving for excellence?

The Macedonian believers gave "as much as they were able, and even beyond their ability" (2 Corinthians 8:3). What does it mean to give *beyond* our ability? It means pushing our giving past the point where the figures add up. It means giving when the bottom line says we can't.

Scott Lewis attended a conference where Bill Bright challenged people to give one million dollars to

What does it mean to give beyond our ability?

help fulfill the great commission. This amount was laughable to Scott—far beyond anything he could imagine since his machinery business was generating an income of under fifty thousand dollars a year.

Bill asked, "How much did you give last year?" Scott felt pretty good about his answer: "We gave seventeen thousand dollars, about 35 percent of our income."

Without blinking an eye, Bill responded, "Over the next year, why don't you make a goal of giving fifty thousand dollars?"

Scott thought Bill hadn't understood. That was more than he had made all year! But Scott and his wife decided to trust God with Bill's challenge, asking Him to do the impossible. God provided in amazing ways. With a miraculous December 31 provision, the Lewises were able to give the fifty thousand dollars. The next year they set a goal of giving one hundred thousand dollars. Again, God provided.

Scott wrote me a note saying that in 2001, they passed the one-million-dollar mark in their giving. The best part is that they aren't stopping. *That's* what it means to excel at giving.

GIVE IT NOW OR GIVE IT LATER?

People ask, "Should I give now, or should I hang on to it, hoping my investments will do well and I'll have more to give in a year or two?"

I respond with two questions of my own: "How soon do you want to experience God's blessing?" and "Do you want to be sure the money goes to God's kingdom, or are you willing to risk that it won't?"

When we stand before God, I don't believe He'll say, "You blew it when you gave Me all that money before the stock market peaked."

I don't believe it's ever wrong to give now. With 10,000 percent interest (Matthew 19:29), God can produce far greater returns on money invested in heaven today than Wall Street or real estate ever can.

I don't believe it's ever wrong to give now.

If we don't give now we run some real risks:

- The economy may change and we'll have less to give. God says we don't know what's going to happen tomorrow (James 4:13–17). Countless investors have been "absolutely sure" about getting great returns on money that disappears overnight.
- Our hearts may change and we may not follow through with giving.

   Zaccheus said, "Here and *now* I give my possessions (emphasis mine)." If you procrastinate, the same heart that's prompting you to give today may later persuade you not to. Why? Because as a result of postponing giving, your heart's vested interests increase on earth and decrease in heaven.

• Our lives may end before we've given what we intended.

You may think, *No problem there. I'm putting my church and ministries in my will.* By all means, do your estate planning and give heavily to God's kingdom. But what kind of trust does it take to part with your money once you die? You don't have any choice!

Death isn't your best opportunity to give; it's the end of your opportunity to give. God rewards acts of faith done while we're still living.

We also need to examine the present worthiness of any organization we give to. I agree with financial advisor Ron Blue, who says, "Do your givin' while you're livin', so you're knowin' where it's goin'."

John Wesley said, "Money never stays with me. It would burn me if it did. I throw it out of my hands as soon as possible, lest it should find its way into my heart." Wesley earned significant book royalties during his life—yet his goal was to give so generously as to leave virtually nothing behind when he died. He achieved his goal. While it still had value, he traded in his "Confederate" currency for treasures in heaven.

When the Lord returns, what will happen to all the money sitting in bank accounts, retirement programs, estates, and foundations? It will burn like wood, hay, and straw, when it could have been given in exchange for gold, silver, and precious stones. Money that could have been used to feed the hungry and fulfill the great commission will go up in smoke.

Have you ever played one of those card games where the winner is the one who runs out of cards first? At the end of the game, every card left counts against you. The American dream is to die with as many cards in your hand as possible. But maybe we've got it backwards. Maybe our strategy should be like John Wesley's—to not get stuck with all those cards at our life's end.

WHAT WILL WE LEAVE THE KIDS?

"What about our children?" you may ask. "Aren't we supposed to leave them all our money?" The answer is no.

Nanci and I will leave to our daughters only enough to be of modest assistance, but not enough to change their lifestyles or undercut their need to plan and pray with and depend on their husbands. We've communicated this, and they understand and agree with our plan to give most of our estate to God's kingdom.

Leaving a large inheritance to children is not just a

missed opportunity to invest in God's kingdom. It's also rarely in the children's best interests.

I've heard countless inheritance horror stories over the years. Study the lives of people who have inherited significant wealth and you'll find that in the vast majority of cases, it's made them more unhappy, greedy, and cynical. Who needs to work hard when you've got all that money? Money funds new temptations, including addictions. Giving money to a careless spender is throwing gasoline on a fire. And nothing divides siblings more quickly than a large inheritance. Leaving more to God's kingdom and less to financially independent children is not just an act of love toward God, but toward them.

In Old Testament times, leaving an inheritance was critical (Proverbs 13:22), because children couldn't afford to buy their own land and could end up enslaved or unable to care for their parents. But today, inheritances are often windfalls coming to people who are financially independent and already have more than they need.

Andrew Carnegie said, "The almighty dollar bequeathed to a child is an almighty curse. No man has the right to handicap his son with such a burden as great wealth."

Your children should love the Lord, work hard, and experience the joy of trusting God. More important than leaving your children an inheritance is leaving them a spiritual heritage. If you left your children money they didn't need, and if they were thinking correctly, wouldn't they give it to God anyway? Then why not give it to God yourself, since He entrusted it to you?

Let God decide how much to provide for your adult children. Once they're on their own, the money you've generated under God's provision doesn't belong to your children—it belongs to Him. After all, if *your* money manager died, what would you think if he left all your money to *his* children?

WHY HAS GOD ENTRUSTED SO MUCH TO US?

Jesus said, "Give, and it will be given to you. A good measure, pressed down, shaken together and running over, will be poured into your lap. For with the measure you use, it will be measured to you" (Luke 6:38).

The more you give, the more comes back to you, because God is the greatest giver in the universe, and He won't let you outgive Him. Go ahead and try. See what happens.

R. G. LeTourneau invented earthmoving machines. He gave away 90 percent of his income. But

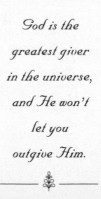

God is the greatest giver in the universe, and He won't let you outgive Him.

the money came in faster than he could give it away. LeTourneau said, "I shovel it out and God shovels it back—but God has a bigger shovel!"

Health and wealth gospel dishonors Christ, since any gospel that is more true in America than China is not the true gospel. Prosperity theology is built on a half-truth. God often *does* prosper givers materially. But He won't let us treat Him like a no-lose slot machine or a cosmic genie who does our bidding. Giving is a sacrifice, and sometimes we will *feel* that sacrifice. God's payoff is very real, but it comes at the "proper time," which may not be today or tomorrow but in eternity (Galatians 6:9).

God has given you considerable material blessings. Have you ever asked yourself, *Why has He provided so much?* You don't need to wonder. Paul tells us exactly why He provides us with more money than we need:

> Now he who supplies seed to the sower and bread for food will also supply and increase your store of seed and will enlarge the harvest of your righteousness. You will be made rich in every way so that... (2 Corinthians 9:10–11)

So that *what?* How will he finish this sentence? Prosperity theology would finish it, "so that we might live in wealth, showing the world how much God blesses those who love Him."

But that isn't how Paul finishes it. He says, "You will be made rich in every way *so that you can be generous on every occasion*" (v. 11, emphasis mine).

Paul is relating the sixth and final key to the Treasure

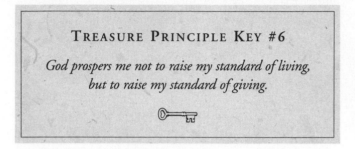

TREASURE PRINCIPLE KEY #6

God prospers me not to raise my standard of living, but to raise my standard of giving.

Principle.

God comes right out and tells us why He gives us more money than we need. It's not so we can find more ways to spend it. It's not so we can indulge ourselves and spoil our children. It's not so we can insulate ourselves from needing God's provision.

It's so we can *give*—generously.

When God provides more money, we often think, *This is a blessing*. Well, yes, but it would be just as scriptural to think, *This is a test*.

The money manager has legitimate needs, and the Owner is generous—He doesn't demand that His stewards live in poverty, and He doesn't resent our making reasonable expenditures on ourselves.

But suppose the Owner sees us living luxuriously in a mansion, driving only the best cars, and flying first-class? Or buying only expensive clothes and electronic gadgets and eating at the best restaurants? Isn't there a point when, as His stewards, we can cross the line of reasonable expenses? Won't the Owner call us to account for squandering money that's not ours?

We don't own the store. We just work here!

❦

We're called God's servants, and we're told it's required of us that we "prove faithful" (1 Corinthians 4:2). We're God's errand boys and delivery girls. We should keep that in mind when we set our salaries. Let's not have an inflated view of our own value. We don't own the store. We just work here!

Suppose you have something important you want to get to someone who needs it. You wrap it up and hand it over to the FedEx guy. What would you think if instead of delivering the package, he took it home, opened it, and kept it for himself?

You'd say, "This guy doesn't get it. The packages don't belong to him. He's just the middleman. His job is to get them from me to the person I want him to hand them off to."

Just because God puts His money in our hands doesn't

mean He intends for it to stay there!

That's what Paul told the Corinthians, encouraging them to give to the needy in Jerusalem:

> At the present time your plenty will supply what they need, so that in turn their plenty will supply what you need. Then there will be equality, as it is written: "He who gathered much did not have too much, and he who gathered little did not have too little." (2 Corinthians 8:14–15)

Why does God give some of His children more than they need and others less than they need? So that He may use His children to help one another. He doesn't want us to have too little or too much (Proverbs 30:8–9). When those with too much give to those with too little, two problems are solved. When they don't, two problems are perpetuated.

God distributes wealth unevenly not because He loves some of His children more than others, but so His children can distribute it to their brothers and sisters on His behalf.

Paul said that the God who supplies seed to the sower will increase our store of seed. Why? So we can stockpile seed or eat it? No, so we can scatter it and spread it out that it might bear fruit. Abundance isn't God's provision for me to live in luxury. It's His provision for me to help others live. God entrusts me with this money not to build my kingdom on earth, but to build His kingdom in heaven.

Are you eager to plant God's money in the field of a world that needs Christ? Does the thought of giving to what will count for eternity make your spine tingle? Does storing up treasures in heaven make your heart leap?

If we understood the out-of-this-world returns, we'd join the Macedonians and beg for the privilege of giving.

God's Royalties

Remember that $8.2 million lawsuit? Recently, the ten-year judgment period expired. Our ministry board said, "Randy, you don't need to earn minimum wage anymore. You can start taking royalties again."

Nanci and I talked and prayed about it. We decided we don't need a higher standard of living. We don't need a better house or car. We don't need a better retirement program or more insurance. So, with joy in our hearts, we said, "No thanks." (Later we discovered the abortion clinic got the judgment extended for another ten years. But we're thankful we didn't know that when we made our decision.)

They're not our book royalties; they're God's. Nanci and I have a certain amount we live on, and we're comfortable. The rest goes to the kingdom. We don't need a million dollars or a hundred thousand dollars. We do fine on a lot less. God provides for us faithfully. And we get to experience one of life's greatest thrills—the joy of giving.

Chapter 6

FOR SUCH A
TIME AS THIS

*It ought to be the business of every day
to prepare for our last day.*

MATTHEW HENRY

Alfred Nobel dropped the newspaper and put his head in
his hands.

It was 1888. Nobel was a Swedish chemist who made
his fortune inventing and producing dynamite. His brother
Ludvig had died in France.

But now Alfred's grief was compounded by dismay.
He'd just read an obituary in a French newspaper—not his
brother's obituary, but *his!* An editor had confused the
brothers. The headline read, "The Merchant of Death Is
Dead." Alfred Nobel's obituary described a man who had

gotten rich by helping people kill one another.

Shaken by this appraisal of his life, Nobel resolved to use his wealth to change his legacy. When he died eight years later, he left more than $9 million to fund awards for people whose work benefited humanity. The awards became known as the Nobel Prizes.

Alfred Nobel had a rare opportunity—to look at the assessment of his life at its end and still have the chance to change it. Before his life was over, Nobel made sure he had invested his wealth in something of lasting value.

FIVE MINUTES AFTER WE DIE

At the end of the movie *Schindler's List,* there's a heart-wrenching scene in which Oskar Schindler—who bought from the Nazis the lives of many Jews—looks at his car and his gold pin and regrets that he didn't give more of his money and possessions to save more lives. Schindler had used his opportunity far better than most. But in the end, he longed for a chance to go back and make better choices.

Unbelievers have no second chance to relive their lives, this time choosing Christ. But Christians also get no second chance to live life over, this time doing more to help the needy and invest in God's kingdom. We have one brief opportunity—a lifetime on earth—to use our resources to make a difference.

John Wesley said, "I judge all things only by the price they shall gain in eternity." Missionary C. T. Studd said, "Only one life, 'twill soon be past; only what's done for Christ will last."

Five minutes after we die, we'll know exactly how we should have lived. But God has given us His Word so we don't have to wait to die to find out. And He's given us His Spirit to empower us to live that way now.

> *Five minutes after we die, we'll know exactly how we should have lived.*

Ask yourself, *Five minutes after I die, what will I wish I would have given away while I still had the chance?* When you come up with an answer, why not give it away now? Why not spend the rest of our lives closing the gap between what we'll wish we would have given and what we really are giving?

Nobel managed to change his legacy in this world. We have the far more strategic opportunity to change our legacy in the world to come.

When you leave this world, will you be known as one who accumulated treasures on earth that you couldn't keep? Or will you be recognized as one who invested treasures in heaven that you couldn't lose?

Put yourself in Alfred Nobel's shoes. Find a piece of paper and a pen. Sit down; think about it; then write your own obituary. Make a list of what you'll be remembered for. Go ahead.

Done? Now read your obituary. How do you feel about it?

Try writing it again, this time from the perspective of heaven, perhaps written by an observing angel. Do you think God is pleased with your earthly life?

Maybe you're living a life that's Christ-centered, with few regrets. Maybe you're daily laying up treasures in heaven.

Or maybe not. If you're like me, you wish heaven's summary of your life were more pleasing to the Audience of One. You may be discouraged by what you've written. If so, don't lose hope. The good news is that you're still here! Like Nobel, you have the opportunity—with God's empowerment—to edit your life, and thereby your obituary, into what you want it to be.

THE GIFT OF GIVING

In Romans 12, Paul lists seven spiritual gifts, including prophecy, serving, teaching, mercy, and giving. I'm convinced that of all these gifts, giving is the one least thought about in the Western church.

Of course, all of us are called to serve, show mercy, and give, even if we don't have those specific gifts. But I believe that in different times of history God has sovereignly distributed certain gifts more widely (such as the gift of mercy during devastating plagues).

Suppose God wanted to fulfill His plan of world evangelization and help an unprecedented number of suffering people. What gift would you expect Him to distribute widely? Perhaps the gift of giving? And what might you expect Him to provide for those to whom He's given that gift? Perhaps unprecedented wealth to meet all those needs and further His kingdom?

Look around. Isn't that exactly what God has done? The question is, what are we doing with the wealth He's entrusted to us to reach the lost and help the suffering?

We regularly see the gift of teaching and know what it looks like. We hear testimonies about miraculous healings, restored marriages, and nearly everything else but giving. We know of prayer warriors and Bible students, but rarely do we hear stories of people giving most of their incomes to the Lord.

It's increasingly common for Christians to ask one another the tough questions: How is your marriage? Have you been spending time in the Word? How are you doing in terms of sexual purity? Have you been sharing your faith? But how often do we ask, "How much are you giving to the Lord?" or "Have you been robbing God?" or "Are you winning the battle against materialism?"

When it comes to giving, churches operate under a "don't ask, don't tell" policy.

❦

When it comes to giving, churches operate under a "don't ask, don't tell" policy. We lack communication, accountability, and modeling. It's as if we have an unspoken agreement: "I won't talk about it if you won't, so we can go right on living as we are."

Think about it. How does a young Christian in the church learn to give? Where can he go to see what giving looks like in the life of a believer captivated by Christ? Why are we surprised when, seeing no other example, he takes his cues from a materialistic society?

We're to "consider how we may spur one another on toward love and good deeds" (Hebrews 10:24). Shouldn't we then be asking how we can spur one another on toward giving?

Some may object, "But we don't want to compare each other's giving." Paul tells the Corinthians of the Macedonians' giving, saying he's making a comparison to motivate them (2 Corinthians 8:7–8). Dixie Fraley told me about some friends of hers. She said, "They're such an example of the art of giving. Every year we try to outgive each other!" Why not? Isn't that spurring one another on? Don't we need to help each other raise the bar of giving so we can learn to jump higher?

Scripture tells us not to give *in order to* be seen by men (Matthew 6:1). Certainly we should be careful to avoid pride. But Jesus also said, "Let your light shine before men, that they may see your good deeds and praise your Father in heaven" (Matthew 5:16). Through an unfortunate misinterpretation of biblical teaching, we've hidden giving under a basket. As a result we're not teaching Christians to give. And they're lacking joy and purpose because of it.

When our missions pastor returned from Sudan, he told our church about enslaved Christians in that region. Spontaneously, several families decided to forgo giving Christmas presents that year and instead give toward freeing slaves. The fourth-grade class at our school raised thousands of dollars for this purpose through work projects. One sixth-grade girl took the fifty dollars she'd saved up to play on a basketball team and gave it to help Sudanese believers.

One family had saved several hundred dollars to go to Disneyland. Their child asked if they could give the money to help the slaves instead. Before long, people had given sixty thousand dollars to redeem slaves. We never even took an offering, but the giving was contagious. People told each other their giving stories. And when they did, it thrilled and encouraged the body to give more. It was one of the church's finest hours, and an essential component was people sharing how God had led them to give.

King David told the people exactly how much he'd

given to build the temple. The precise amounts of gold and precious stones given by the leaders were also made public. "The people rejoiced at the willing response of their leaders, for they had given freely and wholeheartedly to the LORD" (1 Chronicles 29:6–9). The people could rejoice only because they knew what their leaders had given. They could follow their leaders' example in giving only because they knew how much they had given. Unless we learn how to humbly tell each other our giving stories, our churches will not learn to give.

We need to know about the widow at church who lives on a low income and fasts every Thursday, then gives money to the hungry that she would have spent on food. It would have been an incalculable loss to my spiritual life not to hear the stories of Hudson Taylor, George Mueller, Amy Carmichael, and R. G. LeTourneau. They lived as they did to please God, not me, but knowing what God did in them has been an inspiration to let Him do more in me.

A SENSE OF DESTINY

The fact that you're reading these words is likely part of God's plan to change your life—and in turn to change history and eternity.

Remember what Mordecai said to Esther? "If you remain silent at this time, relief and deliverance for the Jews will arise from another place, but you and your father's family will perish. And who knows but that you have come to royal position for such a time as this?" (Esther 4:14).

Just as Esther was in a position of privilege, so is nearly everyone reading this book. Are you educated and literate? Do you have food, clothing, shelter, a car, perhaps some electronic equipment? Then you are among the privileged, the world's wealthy.

Why has God entrusted you with the privilege of wealth? For such a time as this. God has sovereignly raised you up. When I think about our family's resources and the giving opportunities the Lord repeatedly blesses us with, I can't help but feel that we're part of something much larger than our little corner of the world in Oregon.

One ministry calls a group of its key donors History's Handful. Is there an exaggerated sense of significance in this title? I don't think so. Giving to God's great causes infuses us with a sense of destiny. It's no accident that you live in this time and place in history. Remind yourself again why the God of providence has entrusted you with so much: "Your plenty will supply what they need.... You will be made rich...so that you can be generous on every occasion" (2 Corinthians 8:14; 9:11).

It's no accident that you live in this time and place in history.

Is that your destiny? Is God calling you to be a more generous giver? Is He calling you to share with others the liberating joy of the Treasure Principle?

You've heard of prayer warriors. What about giving warriors? God has entrusted us with so much. Perhaps He is raising up a great army of givers, and He's calling us to enlist.

Many today are praying the prayer of Jabez: "Bless me and enlarge my territory!" (1 Chronicles 4:10). Why not pray that prayer about your giving? Why not set a figure you can live on, then tell God that everything He provides beyond that amount you'll give back to Him?

We have no way of knowing how long our nation's prosperity will last. Why not give away the abundance while we still can? Let's give until our hearts are more in touch with God's kingdom work than with our remodeling projects, business ventures, dream vacations, or retirement plans.

Let's ask God if He wants us to hold off from building our dream house here, realizing that our Bridegroom's already building our dream house in heaven. Meanwhile, we can use God's funds to build something that won't go up in smoke, but will last for eternity.

THOUGHTS TO CONSIDER

"How much is God leading me to give in freewill offerings?" Only God can answer that question. That means we need to ask Him. He hasn't established one set amount or percentage for voluntary offerings. Maybe that's precisely so we will need to pray and seek His guidance, which He promises (James 1:5). It's our job to listen and obey.

Giving should start with your local Bible-believing, Christ-centered church, the spiritual community to which you're accountable (Galatians 6:6; 1 Corinthians 9:9–12). Beyond that, you can generously support worthy missions and parachurch ministries, carefully evaluating them by biblical standards.[7]

People ask me, "Should I support secular organizations?" It's fair to ask whether the Humane Society, as good as it may be, is as close to God's heart as evangelism, church planting, or helping the poor in Christ's name. Many people support so-called Christian colleges that no longer believe their doctrinal statements and now lead students astray. With all the godly ministries and schools we could support, why give God's money to institutions that actively oppose His agenda? For every good secular organization there's a Christian organization doing the same work—but with an eternal perspective. When there's a choice, why not support organizations characterized by prayer, biblical standards, and the supernatural work of God's Spirit?

Why not ask God how you might share the Treasure Principle with others? Perhaps you'll be like the people who led D. L. Moody and Billy Graham to Christ—you may influence others to give far more than you ever can.

Consider passing on this book. Sit down with your spouse or friends, and pray about these issues. You could set up a breakfast, Bible study, or discussion group, using this book or Crown Financial Ministries material on money or giving.[8] Ask God to point out those within your unique sphere of influence that you can talk with, study with, or pray with, those you can mentor or be mentored by.

MY GIVING COVENANT

Here's a six-step plan that will help keep you on the Treasure Principle track. It's a giving covenant between you and God. I encourage you to read it, talk it over with your spouse or friends, and pray about it.

If you sense that God is leading you to make a new commitment to giving, I urge you to sign the abbreviated version of the covenant at the end of this book.

1. I affirm God's full ownership of me (1 Corinthians 6:19–20) and everything entrusted to me (Psalm 24:1). I recognize that my money and possessions are in fact His. I'm His money manager, His delivery person. I will ask Him what He wants me to do with His money.

2. I will set aside the firstfruits—starting with at least 10 percent—of all I receive, treating it as holy and belonging exclusively to the Lord. I do this in obedience to Him, desiring His blessing (Malachi 3:6–12). By faith I take God up on His challenge to test Him in this.

3. Out of the remaining treasures God entrusts to me, I will seek to make generous freewill gifts. I recognize that God has entrusted wealth to me so that I can be "generous on every occasion" (2 Corinthians 9:11). Realizing I can rob God by withholding not only the tithe but whatever offerings He calls upon me to give, I ask Him to make His will clear to me.

4. I ask God to teach me to give sacrificially to His purposes, including helping the poor and reaching the lost. I commit myself to avoiding indebtedness so that I don't tie up His funds and can therefore feel greater freedom to follow the Spirit's promptings to give.

5. Recognizing that I cannot take earthly treasures from this world, I determine to lay them up as heavenly treasures—for Christ's glory and the eternal good of others and myself. Affirming that heaven, not earth, is my home and Christ is my Lord, I commit myself to lay out His assets before Him regularly—leaving nothing as untouchable—and ask His direction for

what to do with and where to give His money. I'll start with this question: "What am I hanging on to that You want me to give away?"

6. Recognizing that God has given me my family, my friends, my church, and others in my circle of influence, I ask Him to help me share the Treasure Principle with them so they too may experience the greatest present joy and future reward.

THE GREATEST PLEASURE

There's one statement of Jesus recorded in Acts that doesn't appear in the Gospels. Perhaps God added it later so it would stand out:

> "The Lord Jesus himself said: 'It is more blessed to give than to receive.'" (Acts 20:35)

We're so absorbed with "getting what's ours" that we miss what brings the real blessing and joy—giving God what's His. Giving is doing what we were made for: loving God and our neighbors (Matthew 22:36–40). Giving boldly affirms Christ's lordship. It is a blessed act that leads to joy.

A graphic example of this joy is found in Charles Dickens's classic story *A Christmas Carol.* When the story begins, Ebenezer Scrooge is wealthy and miserable. He's caustic, complaining, and horrendously greedy.

After encounters with three spirits on Christmas Day, he is given a second chance at life. I read this story again recently and was struck by the description of the transformed Scrooge:

> He went to church, and walked about the streets, and watched the people hurrying to and fro, and patted children on the head, and questioned beggars, and looked down into the kitchens of houses, and up to the windows; and found that everything could yield him pleasure. He had never dreamed that any walk—that anything—could give him so much happiness.[9]

After his transformation, Scrooge walks through the streets of London, freely distributing his wealth to the needy. He's giddy with delight. He, who only yesterday had scoffed at the idea of charity, now takes his greatest pleasure in giving.

Scrooge is giddy with delight.

On the story's final page, Dickens says of Scrooge:

> Some people laughed to see the alteration in him, but he let them laugh, and little heeded them.... His own heart laughed, and that was quite enough for him. And it was always said of him, that he

knew how to keep Christmas well, if any man alive possessed the knowledge.[10]

What was the source of Scrooge's transformation? Gaining an eternal perspective. Through supernatural intervention, Scrooge was allowed to see his past, present, and still-changeable future through the eyes of eternity. Let's ask God for the same insight into our lives.

Ebenezer Scrooge leaped for joy on the streets of London because he'd discovered the life-giving antidote to the materialism that had poisoned his soul. Scrooge learned the Treasure Principle—the secret of joyful giving.

Do you want to experience this kind of joy? I invite you to transfer your assests from earth to heaven. I invite you to give humbly, generously, and frequently to God's work. Excel in giving so that you may please God, serve others, and enjoy treasures in heaven.

I urge you to embrace Christ's invitation: "Give, and it will be given to you" (Luke 6:38). Then when He gives you more, remind yourself why: that you may be generous on every occasion.

I invite you to send your treasures on to heaven, where they will safely await you. When you do, you'll feel the freedom, experience the joy, and sense the smile of God.

When you give, you'll feel His pleasure.

Treasure Principle

You can't take it with you—but you *can* send it on ahead.

Treasure Principle Keys

GOD OWNS EVERYTHING. I'M HIS MONEY MANAGER.

We are the managers of the assets God has entrusted—not given—to us.

MY HEART ALWAYS GOES WHERE I PUT GOD'S MONEY.

Watch what happens when you reallocate your money from temporal things to eternal things.

HEAVEN, NOT EARTH, IS MY HOME.

We are citizens of "a better country—a heavenly one" (Hebrews 11:16).

I SHOULD LIVE NOT FOR THE DOT BUT FOR THE LINE.

From the dot—our present life on earth—extends a line that goes on forever, which is eternity in heaven.

GIVING IS THE ONLY ANTIDOTE TO MATERIALISM.

Giving is a joyful surrender to a greater person and a greater agenda. It dethrones me and exalts Him.

GOD PROSPERS ME NOT TO RAISE MY STANDARD OF LIVING, BUT TO RAISE MY STANDARD OF GIVING.

God gives us more money than we need so we can give—generously.

My Giving Covenant

1. I affirm God's full ownership of me and everything entrusted to me.

2. I set aside the firstfruits—at least 10 percent—of every wage and gift I receive as holy and belonging exclusively to the Lord.

3. Out of the remaining treasures God entrusts to me, I seek to make generous freewill gifts.

4. I ask God to teach me to give sacrificially to His purposes, including helping the poor and reaching the lost.

5. Recognizing that I cannot take earthly treasures from this world, I determine to lay them up as heavenly treasures—for Christ's glory and the eternal good of others and myself.

6. I ask God to show me how to lead others to the present joy and future reward of the Treasure Principle.

Signed: _____

Witness: _____

Date: _____

31 RADICAL, LIBERATING QUESTIONS TO ASK GOD ABOUT YOUR GIVING

Asking specific questions of God is a great tradition in Scripture.

Abraham stood by the oaks of Mamre and asked the Lord, "Will not the Judge of all the earth do right?"

At a great hinge point in his life (2 Samuel 2:1–2), David asked the Lord two very specific questions:

> *"Shall I go up to one of the towns of Judah?"* he asked.
> The LORD said, "Go up."
> David asked, *"Where shall I go?"*
> "To Hebron," the LORD answered.
> So David went up.

As God's children, we should ask Him more than just rhetorical questions. We should ask and seek and knock, expecting some kind of response or provision from our God (see Matthew 7:7). The Lord has no trouble handling our most challenging questions. His answers won't always be as unmistakable as they were to David, but He invites us to ask Him nonetheless.

When it comes to financial stewardship, God hasn't handed each of us a standardized checklist with little boxes to mark off one by one. Rather, He has provided us His Word with principles for effective financial stewardship—principles we have to wrestle with. In the process of this struggle, God expects us to seek His face and to pursue the counsel of godly believers who have traveled further than we along Stewardship Road.

God is the owner of all and we are His stewards, His money managers. A responsible steward consults the owner, seeking His direction. Financial stewardship decisions require insight and wisdom beyond our own. Scripture says, "If any of you lacks wisdom, he should ask God, who gives generously to all without finding fault" (James 1:5).

Do you truly desire God's wisdom and empowerment in making difficult stewardship decisions (and evaluating your own heart on the subject)? *Then ask.* He won't leave you in the dark. He has given you His Word and His Spirit to guide you.

The following thirty-one questions are designed to assist you in your quest. (You can ponder consecutively as many as you wish, or meditate on one per day for a month.) After each question, I've listed a key passage of Scripture that has bearing on the issue at hand, as well as other passages I'd encourage you to look up.

God's Word has a power that my words and yours can't come close to matching. He promises that His Word won't return to Him without accomplishing the purpose for which He sent it (see Isaiah 55:11). So in each of these brief meditations, focus first and foremost on the Scriptures and secondarily on the questions.

Ask the Holy Spirit to speak to your heart and give you direction. He will. Count on it.

QUESTIONS TO ASK GOD

1. Time and again in Your Word, Lord, You make a direct connection between experiencing grace and expressing grace through giving. Grace is Your lightning, and giving is our thunder in response. So here's my question: Has the degree of my giving suggested that I have recognized and embraced the full extent of Your grace in my life? Or does it suggest I need to recognize and respond to Your grace in deeper and more heartfelt ways?

   > See that you also excel in this grace of giv-
   > ing.... For you know the grace of our
   > Lord Jesus Christ, that though he was rich,
   > yet for your sakes he became poor, so that
   > you through his poverty might become
   > rich. (2 Corinthians 8:7, 9)

   > See also 2 Corinthians 9:15 and Romans
   > 8:32.

2. Father, could it be that You have raised me up—with the financial assets You've entrusted to me—for just such a time as this? Is it more than a coincidence that You have entrusted me with such resources just at that point in history when an unparalleled number of people have such great needs and there are unprecedented means and opportunities to help them?

> "And who knows whether you have not
> come to the kingdom for such a time as
> this?" (Esther 4:14, ESV)

> See also Acts 17:26 and Ephesians 2:10.

3. Is my life revolving around You? Open my eyes, Father. What am I holding on to that's robbing me of present joy and future reward? What am I guarding and keeping for myself that's preventing me from having to depend wholeheartedly on You? Since money and things have mass, and mass exerts gravity, and gravity holds us in orbit, what can I give away that will bring me greater freedom? Which of "my" assets can I give to You, so that You will be my center of gravity?

> "No servant can serve two masters. Either
> he will hate the one and love the other, or
> he will be devoted to the one and despise
> the other. You cannot serve both God and
> Money." (Luke 16:13)

See also Psalm 42:1–2 and Matthew 5:6.

4. Lord, am I honoring You as owner and CEO/CFO of the assets You've entrusted to my care? Or am I treating You as a mere financial consultant, to whom I pay a fee (2 percent, 10 percent, or…)? Have I been acting as if I own the store and You work for me, rather than recognizing that You own it and I work for You?

> "The land is mine and you are but aliens and my tenants." (Leviticus 25:23)

> See also Deuteronomy 10:14 and 1 Chronicles 29:11–12.

5. Where in my community—or in the whole world—do You want me to go, to see and participate in meeting physical and spiritual needs through Christ-centered ministries? A soup kitchen? The inner city? Prison ministry? Pro-life work? Is a short-term mission trip or long-term service overseas part of Your exciting plan for me and my family?

> "[Josiah] defended the cause of the poor and needy, and so all went well. Is that not what it means to know me?" (Jeremiah 22:16)

> See also Proverbs 28:27 and Romans 10:13–15.

6. Lord, I'm wondering: Why have You entrusted me with greater financial blessings than I once had? I guess I've assumed You've done it to raise my standard of *living*. But now I'm asking, "Is it instead to raise my standard of *giving?*" Do I really see myself as Your delivery person? Or do I assume that because You've put something in my hands, I'm supposed to keep it for myself? (If I hold on to something You wanted me to give, might someone You intended it for go without?)

> You will be made rich in every way so that
> you can be generous on every occasion,
> and….your generosity will result in
> thanksgiving to God. (2 Corinthians 9:11)
>
> See also 2 Corinthians 8:14 and Acts
> 11:29.

7. Lord Jesus, have I overaccumulated? Have I allowed unwise spending and accumulating debt to inhibit my giving to You? Have I said, "There's not enough left to give," while maintaining spending habits that make *sure* there's not enough to give? Am I giving in proportion to Your great blessing of me? Considering that You required three tithes of the poorest Israelite, is it really possible You would expect less of me who lives in comparative wealth, knows the grace of Jesus, and is indwelt and empowered by Your Holy Spirit?

> Honor the LORD with your wealth, with
> the firstfruits of all your crops; then your
> barns will be filled to overflowing, and
> your vats will brim over with new wine.
> (Proverbs 3:9–10)

> See also Proverbs 22:7 and 1 Corinthians
> 16:2.

8. Lord, I've sometimes wondered why You're not blessing
   me more financially. Could it be that I've been spending
   money on myself first, rather than giving You the firstfruits of what You've provided?

> "Is it a time for you yourselves to be living
> in your paneled houses, while this house
> remains a ruin?"
>   Now this is what the LORD Almighty
> says: "Give careful thought to your ways.
> You have planted much, but have har-
> vested little. You eat, but never have
> enough. You drink, but never have your
> fill. You put on clothes, but are not warm.
> You earn wages, only to put them in a
> purse with holes in it."
>   This is what the LORD Almighty says:
> "Give careful thought to your ways. Go up

into the mountains and bring down tim-
ber and build the house, so that I may
take pleasure in it and be honored," says
the LORD. "You expected much, but see, it
turned out to be little. What you brought
home, I blew away. Why?" declares the
LORD Almighty. "Because of my house,
which remains a ruin, while each of you is
busy with his own house. Therefore,
because of you the heavens have withheld
their dew and the earth its crops. I called
for a drought on the fields and the mountains, on the grain, the new wine, the oil
and whatever the ground produces, on
men and cattle, and on the labor of your
hands." (Haggai 1:4–11)

See also Malachi 3:8–11 and Luke 6:38.

9. Lord, You commended the poor widow for giving everything she had to You, leaving nothing for herself. So is it
ever irresponsible for me to give to You now—no matter
what my situation—rather than wait until later? Have I
fallen for the lie that I just don't have enough to give,
despite the fact that the greatest examples of giving in
Scripture were poor people?

Calling his disciples to him, Jesus said, "I
tell you the truth, this poor widow has put

more into the treasury than all the others.
They all gave out of their wealth; but she,
out of her poverty, put in everything—all
she had to live on." (Mark 12:43–44)

See also 2 Corinthians 8:1–4 and
Galatians 6:9–10.

10. Let me know Your mind on this, Father, because it's such
a different way of thinking: Would it honor You if I deter-
mined a basic level of income and assets sufficient to live
on, then simply gave away whatever You provide beyond
that? In the process, would You teach me to be more
grateful and more content?

Whoever loves money never has money
enough; whoever loves wealth is never satisfied with his income. This too is meaningless. As goods increase, so do those who
consume them. And what benefit are they
to the owner except to feast his eyes on
them? The sleep of a laborer is sweet,
whether he eats little or much, but the
abundance of a rich man permits him no
sleep. (Ecclesiastes 5:10–12)

See also Hosea 13:6 and Philippians
4:11–13.

11. Lord Jesus, since financial assets will burn at Your second coming, will the assets, accounts, and holdings I've stored up on earth be wasted if You return in my lifetime? Like those big chests full of Confederate currency left after the Civil War, will it all be worthless? Was Luther right when he said, "Everything I've kept, I've lost, but all that I've given to God I still possess"? Was A. W. Tozer right when he said, "Any temporal possession can be turned into everlasting wealth; whatever is given to Christ is immediately touched with immortality"?

> But the day of the Lord will come like a thief. The heavens will disappear with a roar; the elements will be destroyed by fire, and the earth and everything in it will be laid bare.
>
> Since everything will be destroyed in this way, what kind of people ought you to be? You ought to live holy and godly lives as you look forward to the day of God and speed its coming. That day will bring about the destruction of the heavens by fire, and the elements will melt in the heat. But in keeping with his promise we are looking forward to a new heaven and a new earth, the home of righteousness.
> (2 Peter 3:10–13)

See also Ecclesiastes 5:15 and
1 Corinthians 9:24–25.

12. I need some help thinking this through, Lord. Doesn't the fact that You entrusted Your money to me, not others, indicate You want *me*—during my lifetime—to invest it in eternity, rather than passing along that responsibility to my children? (Shouldn't I let *You* decide what money You want to entrust to them? And in the case of children who've demonstrated lack of wisdom in money management, wouldn't it be mismanagement of Your funds to pass them on?) Once my children have finished college or are working on their own, would inheriting my wealth (beyond items of special sentimental or heritage value) help their eternal perspective and walk with You—or would it be a complicating or even a corrupting influence that could cause them to stumble? Should I, like John Wesley, seek to make my own hands, while I still live, the executors of the greater part of "my" estate?

An inheritance quickly gained at the
beginning will not be blessed in the end.
(Proverbs 20:21)

See also Proverbs 13:11 and 17:26 and
1 Corinthians 4:2.

13. How can I be sure that the assets You've entrusted to me will serve You after I die? How can I know that those to whom I leave these resources will use them to advance Your kingdom? I guess this is the bottom line: If my children are adults and independent, should I just give away now what I can and, when I die, leave most of what remains to my church or missions or ministries that are close to Your heart? Shouldn't I guide my children to look for the inheritance that comes from *Your* hand, not mine? Shouldn't both I and they fix our eyes on the inheritance in heaven that can be enriched through our faithful giving here and now?

> "Come, you who are blessed by my Father; take your inheritance, the kingdom prepared for you since the creation of the world. For I was hungry and you gave me something to eat...." (Matthew 25:34–35)

> See also 1 Peter 1:3–4 and Colossians 3:23–24.

14. Father, what's the eternal downside in giving as much as I can give to You now? In contrast, what's the eternal downside of minimizing my giving or delaying giving until later? Is there really a danger in giving too much too soon? Or is the true danger giving too little too late?

"Whoever can be trusted with very little
can also be trusted with much, and whoever is dishonest with very little will also
be dishonest with much. So if you have
not been trustworthy in handling worldly
wealth, who will trust you with true
riches? And if you have not been trustworthy with someone else's property, who will
give you property of your own?" (Luke
16:10–12)

See also Luke 19:17, Mark 10:29–30, and
2 Corinthians 5:9–11.

15. Okay, Lord, let's say that You're prompting me to give
now. If I delay that giving—for whatever reason—is it
possible I may die before I get a chance to give it later?
(Or might the money disappear before I get around to
giving it?)

"Show me, O LORD, my life's end and the
number of my days; let me know how
fleeting is my life. You have made my days
a mere handbreadth; the span of my years
is as nothing before you. Each man's life is
but a breath."
Man is a mere phantom as he goes to
and fro: He bustles about, but only in

vain; he heaps up wealth, not knowing
who will get it.

"But now, Lord, what do I look for?
My hope is in you." (Psalm 39:4–7)

See also Ecclesiastes 5:13–14 and 8:8.

16. If I don't release my resources now for Your kingdom
causes, will I be in danger of becoming more wrapped
up in earthly, rather than heavenly, treasure? By postponing giving, will my heart become hardened to Your
promptings to give? Will I then leave myself unprepared
for eternity?

> Command those who are rich in this pres-
> ent world not to be arrogant nor to put
> their hope in wealth, which is so uncer-
> tain, but to put their hope in God, who
> richly provides us with everything for our
> enjoyment. Command them to do good,
> to be rich in good deeds, and to be gener-
> ous and willing to share. In this way they
> will lay up treasure for themselves as a firm
> foundation for the coming age, so that
> they may take hold of the life that is truly
> life. (1 Timothy 6:17–19)

See also Matthew 6:21 and Hebrews 3:15.

17. Since I have no choice but to leave money behind when I die, is it really "giving" to designate through my will the distribution of my estate (i.e., *Your* assets temporarily entrusted to me)? Certainly it would be wise to designate funds for noble purposes, but since it involves no sacrifice and requires no trust in You, is it really "giving" in the full sense? Will I rob myself of joy and reward and rob You of my trust by holding on, until death, to significant assets I could have joyfully given to You while still alive?

> Not that I am looking for a gift, but I am looking for what may be credited to your account. (Philippians 4:17)

> See also Hebrews 9:27 and Ephesians 6:8.

18. Father, Wall Street or real estate can't touch the eternal returns of investing in Your kingdom. Who could match Your promise of 10,000 percent (a hundredfold return)? So why are my eyes so often focused on temporary, earthly investments with such pitifully small returns? Lord, please broaden my perspective, increase my faith, and expand my eternal investment mentality.

> Peter answered him, "We have left everything to follow you! What then will there be for us?"
> Jesus said to them, "I tell you the truth, at the renewal of all things, when the Son

of Man sits on his glorious throne, you
who have followed me will also sit on
twelve thrones, judging the twelve tribes of
Israel. And everyone who has left houses
or brothers or sisters or father or mother
or children or fields for my sake will
receive a hundred times as much and will
inherit eternal life." (Matthew 19:27–29)

See also Hebrews 6:10 and 2 Corinthians
4:18.

19. Lord, please help me to see clearly when it comes to *where*
I give Your money. Help me to use discernment to determine which recipients can most benefit from the money
I give, and which are likely to mismanage it. And am I
giving it to causes You truly value most? Opera? Art muse-
ums? The Humane Society? As good as those things may
be, are they as close to Your heart as evangelism, disciple-
ship, church planting, or helping the poor, the disabled,
the imprisoned, and the unborn and their mothers?

And this is my prayer: that your love may
abound more and more in knowledge and
depth of insight, so that you may be able
to discern what is best. (Philippians
1:9–10)

See also 1 Timothy 5:3–5 and Proverbs 14:7.

20. Since You called the rich young ruler to give away all that He had and follow You in faith, is it possible—could it *ever* happen—that You might actually call me to do the same? Have I bothered to even ask You about this? You called Zacchaeus to give away half of all he had. Since I make twice as much money as some people do, might giving away half of what I have be a reasonable Christ-honoring option for me?

> But Zacchaeus stood up and said to the Lord, "Look, Lord! Here and now I give half of my possessions to the poor, and if I have cheated anybody out of anything, I will pay back four times the amount."
> Jesus said to him, "Today salvation has come to this house, because this man, too, is a son of Abraham. For the Son of Man came to seek and to save what was lost." (Luke 19:8–10)

See also Matthew 19:21 and Luke 14:33.

21. If I were to make a list of all the assets You've entrusted to me, Lord, and ask what You want me to give away, is there *anything*—house, car, real estate, retirement funds, bank

accounts—that I'm leaving off the list or treating as untouchable? Am I acting as if not *everything* belongs to You, but only the leftovers, that part I haven't already committed to something else? If I'm not putting everything on the table and asking You what You want me to do with it, am I really Your disciple?

> The earth is the LORD'S, and everything in it, the world, and all who live in it. (Psalm 24:1)

> See also 1 Corinthians 6:19, Psalm 50:12, and Haggai 2:8.

22. Father, You know my heart inside out. Why do I hang on to my possessions with a white-knuckle grip? Am I trying to prove something? Is it about pride? Power? Prestige? Selfishness? Insecurity? Fear? Without realizing it, am I making money my God-substitute? In material pleasure-seeking, am I failing to experience the pleasures that can be found only in You? Do You want me to do something different—maybe *radically* different—to enhance my longing for You and my dependence on You?

> My soul thirsts for You, my flesh yearns for You,
>   In a dry and weary land where there is no water. (Psalm 63:1, NASB)

See also Colossians 3:4–6 and Psalm 34:8.

23. Am I living to hear others say of me, "He's a great success!"—or to have You say to me, "Well done, My good and faithful servant"? When I meet You face-to-face, will I wish I had given away less—or more? God, help me by Your grace to close the gap between what I'm giving now and what I'll one day wish I had given.

> "Watch out! Be on your guard against all kinds of greed; a man's life does not consist in the abundance of his possessions." (Luke 12:15)

> See also 2 Corinthians 8:7 and Acts 10:1–4.

24. Lord, is my fear of health-related catastrophes and old age causing me to hold back my giving? I know you call me to be wise, but have I gone too far, to the point of hoarding and stockpiling instead of trusting? When it comes right down to it, am I hanging on to excess as a backup plan in case You fail me?

> Therefore do not worry about tomorrow, for tomorrow will worry about itself. Each day has enough trouble of its own. (Matthew 6:34)

See also Proverbs 3:5–6 and Philippians
4:6, 19.

25. It's a terrible thought, Father, but are material assets competing with You for lordship over my life? Has my spiritual life—and my family's—been harmed by our wealth and our infatuation with wealth? Is it true that giving is the only antidote to materialism? Have I been giving enough to experience a release from materialism and a joyful liberty from the tyranny of money and things?

> For we brought nothing into the world,
> and we can take nothing out of it. But if
> we have food and clothing, we will be
> content with that. People who want to get
> rich fall into temptation and a trap and
> into many foolish and harmful desires that
> plunge men into ruin and destruction. For
> the love of money is a root of all kinds of
> evil. Some people, eager for money, have
> wandered from the faith and pierced
> themselves with many griefs. But you,
> man of God, flee from all this, and pursue
> righteousness. (1 Timothy 6:7–11)

> See also Ezekiel 28:4–5 and Revelation
> 3:17–18.

26. What specifically am I hanging on to that You want me to give away? Since You promise me, "It is more blessed [happy-making] to give than to receive," what blessings and happiness am I robbing myself of by holding on to what You want me to give away?

> A generous man will himself be blessed,
> for he shares his food with the poor.
> (Proverbs 22:9)

> See also Acts 20:35 and 2 Corinthians 8:13–15.

27. Please show me, Jesus: How can I better communicate with and pray with my spouse and children so we can walk together down this exhilarating road of giving? Help us, Lord, to both lead and encourage one another, without leaving each other behind.

> A prudent wife is from the LORD.
> (Proverbs 19:14)

> See also 2 Corinthians 9:7 and Ephesians 5:22, 25.

28. What am I doing—and what *should* I be doing—to train my children to be regular, joyful, and generous givers?

> Train a child in the way he should go, and
> when he is old he will not turn from it.
> (Proverbs 22:6)

See also 1 Corinthians 11:1 and 16:2.

29. Lord, I realize that in most places around the world, in most eras of history, I would be regarded as extremely wealthy (even if I am lower- or middle-class in this place and time). Have You put so much into my hands because You have blessed me with the gift of giving and want me to learn to use that gift for Your glory? Have I been missing out on blessing and joy by not exercising this gift?

> In Christ we who are many form one
> body, and each member belongs to all the
> others. We have different gifts, according
> to the grace given us. If a man's gift is
> prophesying, let him use it in proportion
> to his faith. If it is serving, let him serve; if
> it is teaching, let him teach; if it is encour-
> aging, let him encourage; if it is contribut-
> ing to the needs of others, let him give
> generously. (Romans 12:5–8)

See also 2 Corinthians 9:7 and Galatians
6:9.

30. If I am a giver, who have I been teaching and *mentoring* in giving? In a spirit of humility, how can I share with others the joy of giving? If some of us are prayer warriors called to teach others how to pray, are others of us to be *giving warriors?* Are you calling some to be examples who show others how to give and stir them to raise the bar of giving? (Should I aspire to become a giving warrior, and/or seek the counsel and guidance of one?)

> And now, brothers, we want you to know about the grace that God has given the Macedonian churches. Out of the most severe trial, their overflowing joy and their extreme poverty welled up in rich generosity…. For I know your eagerness to help, and I have been boasting about it to the Macedonians, telling them that since last year you in Achaia were ready to give; and your enthusiasm has stirred most of them to action. (2 Corinthians 8:1–2; 9:2–3)

> See also 1 Chronicles 29:1–14 and Hebrews 10:24.

31. Five minutes after I die, what will I wish I had given away while I still had the chance? Father, surely I don't have to wait till I die to figure this out. Please show me now, while I still can give to causes close to Your heart—while I can

experience the joy of knowing others are being fed and helped and reached with the gospel, receiving from my hands the help they need. Please empower me to live each day, the rest of my life here, looking forward to heaven and storing up treasures there. Help me to anticipate the words I long to hear from You: "Well done, good and faithful servant.... Enter into the joy of your Lord" (Matthew 25:21, NKJV).

> For the Son of Man is going to come in
> his Father's glory with his angels, and then
> he will reward each person according to
> what he has done. (Matthew 16:27)

> See also Proverbs 19:17 and Matthew
> 10:42.

ENDNOTES

1. Randy Alcorn, *In Light of Eternity* (Colorado Springs, Colo.: WaterBrook, 1999).

2. John Bunyan, as quoted by Bruce Wilkinson in "Walk Thru Eternal Rewards" seminar notebook, Walk Thru the Bible Ministries.

3. A. W. Tozer, "The Transmutation of Wealth," *Born After Midnight* (Harrisburg, Penn.: Christian Publications, 1959), 107.

4. If you'd like one of these cards at no charge, send a self-addressed, stamped envelope to Eternal Perspective Ministries, 39085 Pioneer Blvd., Suite 206, Sandy, OR 97055.

5. C. S. Lewis, *The Weight of Glory* (New York: Macmillan, 1949), 3–4.

6. Barna Research Update, June 5, 2001; www.barna.org.

7. Randy Alcorn, "Nineteen Questions to Ask before You Give to Any Ministry," Eternal Perspective Ministries, resources/2010/Mar/26/nineteen-questions-ask-you-give-any-organization/.

8. For a selection of these Bible studies, contact Crown Financial Ministries at www.crown.org, 770-534-1000.

9. Charles Dickens, *A Christmas Carol* (Philadelphia, Penn.: The John C. Winston Company, 1939), 128.

10. Ibid, 131.

Resources to Help You with
Giving and Money Management

RONALD BLUE & COMPANY
www.ronblue.com
800-841-0362

CHRISTIAN LEADERSHIP
ALLIANCE
www.christianleadershipalliance.
org
949-487-0900

CROWN FINANCIAL
MINISTRIES
www.crown.org
800-722-1976

ETERNAL PERSPECTIVE
MINISTRIES
www.epm.org
(includes articles by Randy
Alcorn)
503-668-5200

THE GATHERING
www.thegathering.com
903-509-9911

GENEROUS GIVING
www.generousgiving.org

THE GOOD STEWARD
www.thegoodsteward.com
866-364-9980

INTERNATIONAL STEWARD
www.internationalsteward.org
616-734-0950

THE STEWARDSHIP
ALLIANCE
812-386-9170

NATIONAL CHRISTIAN
FOUNDATION
www.nationalchristian.com
800-681-6223

THE TIMOTHY PLAN
www.timothyplan.com
800-846-7526

STEWARDSHIP PARTNERS
www.stewardshippartners.com
800-930-6949

About the Author

RANDY ALCORN is an author and the founder of Eternal Perspective Ministries (EPM), a nonprofit ministry dedicated to teaching principles of God's Word and assisting the church in ministering to the unreached, unfed, unborn, uneducated, unreconciled, and unsupported people around the world. "My ministry focus is communicating the strategic importance of using our earthly time, money, possessions, and opportunities to invest in need-meeting ministries that count for eternity," Alcorn says. "I do that by trying to analyze, teach, and apply the implications of Christian truth."

Before starting EPM in 1990, Randy served as a pastor for fourteen years. He holds degrees in theology and biblical studies, and has taught on the adjunct faculties of Multnomah University and Western Seminary in Portland, Oregon.

Randy has written more than forty books, including the best-sellers *Heaven, The Treasure Principle,* and the Gold Medallion winner *Safely Home.*

He resides in Gresham, Oregon with his wife, Nanci. They have two married daughters and are the proud grandparents of five grandsons. Randy enjoys hanging out with his family, biking, tennis, research, and reading.

You may contact Eternal Perspective Ministries at www.epm.org or 39085 Pioneer Blvd., Suite 206, Sandy, OR 97055 or 503.668.5200. Follow Randy on Facebook: www.facebook.com/randyalcorn, Twitter: www.twitter.com/randyalcorn, and on his blog: www.epm.org/blog.

God. Goodness. Evil. Suffering.

How do they fit together in a way that makes sense?

In this persuasive new book, Randy Alcorn brings a fresh, realistic, and thoroughly biblical approach to dealing with all the issues surrounding the greatest question of human history: Why would a good God allow suffering and evil?

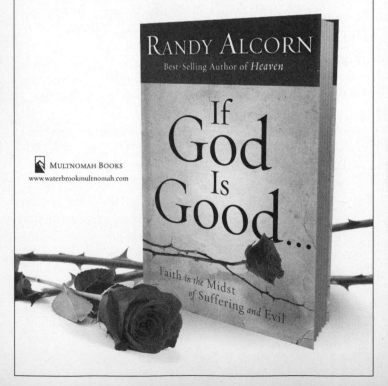

Nonfiction titles from **RANDY ALCORN**

THE TREASURE PRINCIPLE BIBLE STUDY:
Unlocking the Secret of Joyful Giving
Ready for a revolution in material freedom that will utterly change your quality of life? Dig into the companion Bible study to Randy Alcorn's best-selling book.

THE PURITY PRINCIPLE:
God's Safeguards for Life's Dangerous Trails
God has placed warning signs and guardrails to keep us from plunging off the cliff. Find straight talk about sexual purity in Randy Alcorn's one-stop handbook for you, your family, and your church.

THE GRACE AND TRUTH PARADOX:
Responding with Christlike Balance
Living like Christ is a lot to ask! Discover Randy Alcorn's two-point checklist of Christlikeness—and begin to measure everything by the simple test of grace and truth.

PROLIFE ANSWERS TO PROCHOICE ARGUMENTS
This revised and updated guide offers timely information and inspiration from a "sanctity of life" perspective. Real answers to real questions appear in logical and concise form.

Fiction
from Randy Alcorn

DECEPTION
Homicide detective Ollie Chandler has seen it all. But when he's called to investigate the murder of a Portland State University professor, all the evidence is pointing to one horrific conclusion: The murderer is someone in his own department.

DOMINION
When two murders drag a columnist into the world of gangs and racial conflict, he seeks revenge for the killings, and answers to the hard issues regarding race and faith.

DEADLINE
After tragedy strikes those closest to him, journalist Jake Woods is drawn into a complex murder investigation that forces him to ultimately seek answers to the meaning of his existence.

THE ISHBANE CONSPIRACY
Four college students have worse troubles than mid-terms to contend with: A demonic contingent is after their souls.

LORD FOULGRIN'S LETTERS
Lord Foulgrin's Letters invites believers to eavesdrop on their worst Enemy, learn his strategies and tricks, and discover how to ward off his devilish attacks.

Other Books by Randy Alcorn